30秒でできる! ニッポン紹介 おもてなしの英会話

安河内哲也＝監修

IBC

IBC PUBLISHING

本書の音声ダウンロードは
弊社ホームページから！

www.ibcpub.co.jp/shokai/

装　　幀 = 斉藤 啓
本文イラスト = 高橋正輝
編 集 協 力 = David Satterwhite、Robb Satterwhite、佐藤誠司

はじめに

　日本にやってくる外国人の数がどんどん増えています。みなさんも、街の中で困っている外国人をみかけることが多くなったと思います。また、街で外国人に質問されることもあるでしょう。

　私たち日本人が昔から大切にしてきた美徳のひとつは「助け合いの精神」です。でも、困っている外国人を助けたいと思っても、言葉のせいでお手伝いすることができない。そんな経験を持っている方も多いのではないでしょうか？

　英語圏の人々はもちろんですが、多くの訪日外国人はある程度の英語が理解できます。難しい英語を話す必要はまったくありません。おもてなしには、簡単な英語が話せれば十分です。

　本書では、簡単に短く、1トピックのうち1つの質問につき30秒で、日本のことを説明するための英語が収録されています。これだけの英語を勉強しておけば、あなたは立派なニッポンナビゲーターです。

　本書で勉強すれば、もう街で困っている外国人を見かけても素通りすることはないでしょう。まずは笑顔で「こんにちは。Are you okay?（大丈夫ですか）May I help you?（お手伝いしましょうか）」と話しかけてみましょう。そして、相手との会話が始まったら、Welcome to Japan.（日本へようこそ）そして、会話の終わりには、Enjoy your stay. Have a nice day.（滞在を楽しんでください。良い一日を）で相手を送り出しましょう。

　せっかく外国から、はるばる日本に来ていただいたのだから、すこしでも楽しんで帰っていただきたい。そして、私たちの文化に触れていただいて、良い思い出をつくっていただきたい。そんな私たちの気持ちを、本書の英語を学ぶことによって、一人でも多くの人に伝えていきましょう。

2016年7月　六本木にて
安河内哲也

知っておくと便利な「おもてなしの基本表現」

　まずは、外国人に話しかけて、会話をスタートするための基本表現を勉強しましょう。これらの会話を使うときに大切なのが、笑顔です。スマイルこそがコミュニケーションの基本です。英語自体が多少間違っていても、こちらが笑顔であることで、悪い意図はないのだということを伝えることができます。そのようなボディランゲージも大切にしながら会話をしてくださいね。また、相手もせっかく日本に来ているのですから、あいさつくらいは日本語でゆっくり「こんにちは」と話しかけてみるのもよいでしょう。おもてなしの基本は笑顔と度胸です。まずは、基本の英会話の勉強から始めましょう。

※ J＝日本人，F＝外国人

Welcome to Japan. （日本へようこそ）

J　Welcome to Japan. I'm a volunteer sightseeing guide.
（日本へようこそ。私はボランティアの観光ガイドです）

F　Could you tell me where the ticket office is?
（切符売り場はどこにあるか教えていただけますか）

＊相手に歓迎の意を伝えるときの言い方。Welcome to my home [company].（わが家［社］へようこそ）のように使います。

Do you speak English?（あなたは英語を話しますか）

J Do you speak English?
（あなたは英語を話しますか）

F Yes, a little.
（ええ，少し）

＊外国からの旅行者などと話をするには，まず相手が英語を話せるかどうかを尋ねましょう。Can you ～?「～できますか」よりも Do you ～?「（ふだん）～しますか」と尋ねる方が無難です。

Would you like ～?（～はいかがですか）

J Would you like a guide around here?
（このあたりをご案内しましょうか）

F Yes, please.
（ええ，お願いします）

＊「～をご希望ですか」と相手にたずねるときの言い方。What would you like for dinner?「夕食は何を食べたいですか」のようにも使えます。

This is ～ / That is ～（これは～です／あれ［それ］は～です）

F What's that?
（それは何ですか）

J This is a security camera.
（これは防犯カメラです）

＊自分に近いものは this「これ」，自分から遠いものは（相手に近いものも）that「あれ，それ」で表します。

Are you okay?（だいじょうぶですか）/ Can I help you?（どうしましたか）

J You look sick. Are you okay?
（具合が悪そうですね。だいじょうぶですか）

F I'm OK, thank you.
（だいじょうぶです，ありがとう）

＊相手の体調などを気遣うときに使う表現。Are you all right? とも言います。

J Excuse me. Can I help you?
（すみません。どうかなさいましたか［お助けしましょうか］）

F Yes, please. I can't open this door.
（ええ，お願いします。このドアが開かないのです）

＊ Can I help you? は「いらっしゃいませ」などの意味でも使いますが，困っている人を見かけたときに使うこともできます。

Like this.（こんなふうに）

J Please turn the handle. Like this.
（取っ手を回してください。こんなふうに）

F Sure.
（わかりました）

＊like this [that] は「この［その］ように」の意味。何かの動作をするように言われたとき，Like this?（こうですか？）と応答することもできます。

Let me try. （私がやってみましょう）

F Excuse me. I can't use this remote.
（すみません。このリモコンが使えないのですが）

J OK. Let me try.
（わかりました。私がやってみましょう）

＊Let me ～は「私に～させてください」という意味。Let me introduce myself.「自己紹介させてください」のように，me の後ろに動詞を置いて使います。

Be careful. （気をつけて）

J Be careful. That knife is very sharp.
（気をつけて。そのナイフはとてもよく切れますよ）

F Thank you.
（ありがとう）

＊Be で始まる文は「～でありなさい」という命令や忠告の意味を表します。Be quiet, please. は「静かにしてください」です。

I'll show you the way.（道をご案内します）/ This way, please.（こちらです）

F Excuse me. I'm looking for the tourist information center.
（すみません。観光案内所を探しているのですが）

J Sure. I'll show you the way.
（わかりました。道をご案内します）

＊相手を特定の場所まで連れて行くときに使う言い方。「駅までの道」なら the way to the station です。

F Where is the waiting room?
（待合室はどこですか）

J This way, please.
（こちらへどうぞ）

＊これも相手を特定の場所まで連れて行くときに使う言い方。相手が自分で行くよう伝えるときは Down there.「あちらです」などを使います。

You look great.（よくお似合いです）

F How do I look in this hat?
（この帽子は私に似合いますか）

J You look great.
（よくお似合いですよ）

＊ look great は「すばらしく見える」ということ。I like that hat (of yours).「その（あなたの）帽子が気に入りました［その帽子はすてきですね］」などとも言います。

Wait a minute, please.（少しお待ちください）

F Do you have time?
（時間がありますか）

J Wait a minute, please.
（少しお待ちください）

＊相手を少し待たせるときに使う言い方。Just a minute [moment], please. などとも言います。

Have a nice day.（さようなら）／
Have a nice trip.（行ってらっしゃい）

F Thank you for all your help.
（いろいろお世話になりました）

J My pleasure. Have a nice trip.
（どういたしまして。行ってらっしゃい［よい旅を］）

＊別れるときの決まり文句です。金曜日の退社時には同僚に Have a good weekend.「お疲れ様でした［よい週末を］」などと言います。

目次

はじめに　3
知っておくと便利な「おもてなしの基本表現」　4

第1章　日本人の佇まい　15

1　着物 16
2　日本家屋 18
　コラム　日本の家屋の中はどうなっているの？.. 20
3　暖簾 24
4　提灯 26

第2章　日本の象徴　29

1　天皇 30
2　富士山 32
3　神社 34
4　仏教 36
　コラム　神道と仏教のつながり 38
5　禅 40
6　侍 42
7　城 44
8　侘び・寂び・幽玄 46

Contents

第3章　日本の食　㊾

1　寿司 50
2　刺身 52
3　天婦羅 54
4　焼き鳥 56
5　とんかつ 58
6　懐石 60
7　うなぎ 62
8　そば 64
9　ラーメン 66
10　カレーライス 68
11　お好み焼き 70
12　どんぶりもの 72
13　弁当 74
14　梅干し・わさび・鰹節 76
15　お茶 78
16　和菓子 80
17　酒 82
18　焼酎 84

第4章　日本の風物　87

1 花見 88
2 満員電車 90
3 新幹線 92
4 電子マネー 94
5 デパ地下 96
6 コンビニ 98
7 温泉 100
8 旅館 102
9 居酒屋 104
10 だるま 106
11 招き猫 108
12 タクシー 110
13 オタク文化 112
14 コスプレ 114
15 歌謡曲 116

第5章　日本の伝統文化　119

1 歌舞伎 120
2 能 122
3 狂言 124
4 いけばな 126
5 茶道 128
　コラム 茶の湯 130
6 相撲 138
7 盆栽 140
8 浮世絵 142

第6章　日本の都市　145

1　東京 146
2　京都 148
3　大阪 150
4　奈良 152
5　広島 154
6　福岡 156
7　沖縄 158
8　北海道 160
9　銀座 162
10　浅草 164
　　コラム 合羽橋道具街・浅草寺 166

第7章　東京サバイバル　169

1　地下鉄を乗りこなす 170
2　JRを乗りこなす 176
3　成田空港VS羽田空港 178
4　東京の歩き方 182
5　治安 184
6　郵便、キャッシング、
　　クレジットカード 186
7　外国人からよく聞かれる質問 187

第1章

日本人の佇まい

1 着物

❓ こんな質問をされたら？

1 How are kimonos produced?

着物はどうやって仕立てられるの？

2 Is it easy to wear a kimono?

着物は簡単に着られるの？

3 On what sorts of occasions do Japanese people wear a kimono?

日本人はどのような場面で着物を装うの？

Kimono

💬 30秒で、こう答えよう！

1 The production of kimonos requires skilled artisanship, with techniques that are passed on through the generations.

着物を仕立てるには、先代から受け継がれる熟練の技が必要です。

2 Tying the obi on a kimono is quite challenging to do by oneself, so the person wearing a kimono will usually need help to do it properly.

帯を自分で結ぶのはかなり大変で、着物を着る人はたいてい誰かに助けてもらいます。

3 Although Japanese people wear Western clothing in everyday life, they wear kimonos for special occasions such as weddings, funerals, graduation ceremonies and so on.

日本人は日常生活では洋服を着ていますが、結婚式、葬儀、卒業式など特別な場合に着物を着ます。

2 日本家屋

❓ こんな質問をされたら？

1 What is a traditional Japanese-style house like?

伝統的な日本家屋はどのようなものですか？

2 What is the floor made of?

床は何でできていますか？

3 What are the doors that lead to rooms from the house's hallways called?

廊下と部屋を仕切っているドアを何といいますか？

Japanese Style Home

第1章 日本人の住まい

 30秒で、こう答えよう！

1. Traditional Japanese houses are made from wood, with tatami-mat floors and rooms partitioned by shoji screens and *fusuma* sliding doors.

   伝統的な日本家屋は木造で、畳を敷き、障子や襖で部屋が仕切られています。

2. *Tatami* mats, covered with woven soft rush straw, are traditionally used for flooring.

   畳は柔らかい草を織ってつくられます。

3. The doors and room dividers are called shoji, which are wooden frames covered with *washi*, thin Japanese paper.

   障子と呼ばれ、木の枠を薄い和紙で覆ってつくられています。

Column 日本の家屋の中はどうなっているの？

Entrance 玄関

You enter through a sliding door that clatters as you open it. You take off your footwear and step up on to the raised wooden floor called the *agariguchi*. It is good manners to rearrange your shoes so the toes are pointing towards the door.

ガラガラという音を立てる引き戸を開けて入る。履き物を脱いで、一段高い板張りの「あがり口」に上がる。脱いだ履き物は、つま先を入口の方に向けて揃え直すのが礼儀。

Japanese-style rooms 和室

Rooms are laid with tatami mats, the number of which determine the room size of the room, as in 6-mat rooms, 8-mat rooms and so forth. Old Japanese houses were devised so that sliding doors could be removed to create larger rooms as necessary.

畳敷きの部屋で、その数によって6畳間、8畳間などと呼ばれる。古い日本家屋の場合は、必要に応じて各部屋を仕切る襖を取り外すと、広い部屋になるという工夫がこらされている。

Japanese-style toilets 和式トイレ

Unlike Western toilets, on which you sit over the bowl, in Japanese toilets you squat over the bowl with your back to the door. Men can stand over them to urinate. For people used to Western-style toilets, they can come as a bit of a shock.

便器に腰を掛ける欧米式と違い、和式は入口を背にして便器にまたがり用を足す。男性の小用は立ったまま行う。欧米式に慣れた人には、ちょっとしたカルチャーショックだ。

What are Japanese Homes like?

Tokonoma alcove 床の間

The *tokonoma* is an alcove slightly raised from floor level in which an ornament or flower vase is placed, with a painting or piece of calligraphy hung on the wall. They can be seen in tearooms, and even a Japanese-style room in a new house will have a *tokonoma*.

床を一段高くして置物や花瓶を置き、壁に書画などを掛ける。茶室にもみられるもので、新しい日本家屋の和室の一室は必ず床の間つきになっている。

Furo bath 風呂

In old Japanese houses even the bath was made of wood, but nowadays these have all but disappeared. However, the way of bathing remains unchanged, and you should never wash yourself while in the tub.

古い日本家屋は風呂も木製だったが、現在はめっきり見かけなくなった。しかし、入浴法は昔のままで、身体を洗う時は浴槽から出て洗うのが日本流である。

Shoji paper screen 障子

These are screens made of a wooden frame onto which *washi* paper is pasted, and they are good for allowing in natural light and keeping the room warm. They are unique to Japanese houses.

木組みをほどこした戸に和紙を張ったもので、自然の採光や室内の保温に適している。日本家屋ならではの独特の工夫である。

Amado shutter 雨戸

These are shutters that are opened during the day and stored away in built-in compartments, and pulled closed to cover windows at night. They are called *amado*, or "rain doors," since they used to be kept closed on rainy days, but now their main function is to prevent burglaries and maintain privacy.

　日中は収納しておいて、夜は「戸袋」から引き出して使う。雨の日に閉めたことから「雨戸」というが、現在は防犯やプライバシーを守ることが主な役目になっている。

Oshiire cupboard 押入れ

These are the large built-in cupboards in Japanese-style rooms where bedding and items not in daily use are stored. In the past children used to hide in them when scolded by their parents.

　寝具や日常使わないものの保管場所として、和室に付設されている。昔の日本の子供は、親に叱られると、ここに逃げ込んだものだ。

Bedding 寝具

This is the bedding used in a Japanese-style room. All Japanese people used to sleep on a futon mattress laid out on the tatami. At night, the living room was thus quickly converted into a bedroom.

　和室に布団を敷いて寝るのが、昔の日本人の一般的風習だった。夜になると、和室は寝室に早変わりする。

Butsudan Buddhist altar 仏壇

Even today, many people start the day by putting their hands together in prayer before the family's Buddhist altar containing the ancestral memorial tablet.

先祖の位牌を祀った仏壇に向かって手を合わせ、一日のスタートをする日本人が多い。

Kamidana Shinto altar 神棚

Most households involved in trades such as shopkeeping, farming, or fishing keep a shrine dedicated to their patron god.

商売をしている家、農家、漁師の家などは、たいがい神様を祀る神棚を設けている。

Kotatsu heated table こたつ

The whole family gathered around a warm *kotatsu*—a low table heated from below and covered by a quilt—used to be a typical winter scene in Japan. Family breakdown is perhaps not unrelated to the fact that the *kotatsu* has largely been replaced by central heating.

家族全員がこたつに入って暖をとるのが、日本の冬の当たり前の家庭風景だった。家庭崩壊は、暖房の発達でこたつが不要になったことと無縁ではないのかもしれない。

3 暖簾

❓ こんな質問をされたら？

1 What is the small curtain that hangs in shop entrances?

店の入り口にかかっている小さなカーテンのようなものは何ですか？

2 What is printed on it?

その上には何がプリントされているのですか？

3 What is the purpose of hanging it in the entrance?

入り口にかけるのはなぜですか？

Noren

 30秒で、こう答えよう！

1. It's called a *noren*, and it's hung in the entrance of traditional restaurants, shops and public bath houses.

   暖簾といわれるもので、和食店や商店、銭湯などの入り口にかけられています。

2. The name of the establishment (the *yago*), and sometimes a family crest (*mon*) are usually printed on the *noren*.

   ふつう、店の称号（屋号）や家の紋章（紋）が印刷されています。

3. Originally *noren* curtains were simply pieces of cloth that provided shade and helped keep dust from the street from coming in through the door. When a *noren* curtain is hung in the doorway it indicates that the shop is open for business.

   日除けやほこり除けに用いた1枚の布がはじまりです。外に暖簾がかかっているときは、営業中の印です。

4 提灯

❓ こんな質問をされたら？

1 What is this paper lantern?

この紙製の手提げランプのようなものは何ですか？

2 What is it made of?

何でできていますか？

3 Is there anything special about the red ones with writing on them?

何か書かれている赤い色のものは、特別なものですか？

Chochin

 30秒で、こう答えよう！

1 It's called a *chochin*, and it can be hung from a building's eaves, or it can be carried.

提灯といわれるもので、軒下にぶら下げられたり、携行することができます。

2 They are generally made from very strong paper that's attached to collapsible bamboo hoops.

通常、折りたためる輪状の竹ひごに丈夫な和紙を貼り付けてつくります。

3 The red lanterns are called *akachochin*, and the writing usually indicates the shop's name or the type of food served.

赤提灯といい、店名や出される食べ物を知らせています。

第2章

日本の象徴

1 天皇

❓ こんな質問をされたら？

1 What is the role of the Japanese emperor?
天皇の役割とはどのようなものですか？

2 What is the emperor called in Japanese?
日本語でエンペラーのことを何といいますか？

3 Where does the emperor live?
天皇はどこに住んでいますか？

30

The Emperor

💬 30秒で、こう答えよう！

1 According to the constitution, the emperor serves as a symbol of Japan. Just as with the British monarchy, the Japanese emperor has no political role in the country.

憲法では、天皇は日本の象徴であると規定されています。イギリスの王室と同じように、日本の天皇にも政治的なパワーはありません。

---

2 The emperor is referred to as *Tenno* in Japanese. It literally means "Emperor from Heaven."

エンペラーのことを日本では天皇といいます。それは「天からきた皇帝」という意味です。

---

3 The emperor lives in the Imperial Palace, known as *Kokyo* in Japanese, which stands on the former site of Edo Castle.

天皇は皇居という宮廷に住んでいます。それはかつての江戸城におかれています。

第2章 日本の象徴

2 富士山

❓ こんな質問をされたら？

1 Which is the highest mountain in Japan?

日本一高い山は何ですか？

2 Where is it located?

それはどこにありますか？

3 Does it have any special features?

何か特徴はありますか？

💬 30秒で、こう答えよう！

1 It's Mount Fuji, which is 3,776 (three thousand, seven hundred and seventy-six) meters tall.

富士山で標高3776メートルです。

2 It is located along the border between Shizuoka and Yamanashi prefectures.

静岡県と山梨県の境にあります。

3 Mount Fuji has a beautiful, nearly perfect volcanic-cone shape. It is regarded as a symbol of Japan, and it was designated a World Heritage Site in 2013.

富士山は美しく雄大な火山として日本の象徴になっています。2013年に世界遺産に認定されました。

3 神社

❓ こんな質問をされたら？

1 What is Japan's native religion?

日本固有の宗教は何ですか？

2 How often do Japanese people go to shrines to worship?

日本人はどのくらいの頻度で神社に参拝するのですか？

3 What are those big gates in front of every shrine?

神社の前にあるあの大きな門は何ですか？

Jinja

💬 **30秒で、こう答えよう！**

1 The native religion is called Shinto, and places of worship are called *jinja*, or shrines.

それは神道です。礼拝するところは神社と呼ばれます。

2 It depends on the individual, but generally people visit Shinto shrines to pray for good luck and health during the New Year's holiday.

人によって違いますが、日本人はふつうお正月に幸運や健康を祈願するために神社を参拝します。

3 The gates are called *torii*, and they indicate the entrance to a Shinto shrine.

あの門は鳥居といい、神社の入り口を示しています。

4 仏教

❓ こんな質問をされたら？

1 How many Buddhists are there in Japan?

日本には仏教徒は何人いますか？

2 What is the role of Buddhism in modern Japan?

現代の日本において、仏教の役割とは何ですか？

3 Why do visitors to Senso-ji burn incense?

浅草寺の参拝客はなぜお香を炊くのですか？

Buddhism

💬 30秒で、こう答えよう！

1 About 91 million people in Japan identify themselves as Buddhists.

およそ9100万人の日本人が、自分は仏教徒だといいます。

2 For many Japanese people today, Buddhism is mainly related to funeral rituals. Nevertheless, Buddhism has had a profound influence on modern Japan.

皮肉なことに多くの日本人にとって、仏教は今や葬式のためだけにあるといわれています。しかし、仏教が日本に深い影響を及ぼしていることもまた真実です。

3 Visitors light incense sticks as ritual offerings, and they wave smoke over themselves as a purification ritual.

参拝客は、お供えとして線香をあげ、お清めとして煙を自分に扇ぎかけます。

Column 神道と仏教のつながり

なぜ日本人は、神社にも寺にも行くのですか?

　基本的に、宗教に関して言えば、日本人は排他的ではありません。神も仏もその他の精霊も、わたしたち人間にご利益をもたらしてくれる存在です。ですから日本人の多くは、神社で健康を祈願し、新年に寺にお参りし、キリスト教式の結婚式を挙げることも平気です。日本人にとって、それはまったく矛盾してはいないのです。

　しかし、こうしたことがふつうに行われていることを理解するのは大切です。さまざまな"宗教的"行事に参加するために、特定の信仰や宗派に対する義務や献身は求められません。ただ単に助けやご利益や保護を求め、感謝の気持ちを表すために祈り、儀式を行い、祝詞やお経を唱え、神社仏閣を訪れます。歴史を通じて、日本人はそうしてきました。そして今も、その伝統を守り続けています。

神社と寺院が同じ場所に建っていることがあるのはなぜですか?

　7世紀に仏教が日本で広まってまもなく、日本人は仏と神を結びつける方法を模索しはじめました。まず、土地を守護する氏神が仏教の守護神として考えられるようになりました。10世紀には、神は仏や菩薩が姿を変えて現れたものであるとされ、13世紀になると主要な神社の祭神の多くが、特定の仏の化身として同一視されるようになりました。

　こうした神仏の同一視から生まれた思想が、本地垂迹です。仏が日本の神々の姿をとって地上に降りてくることを意味しています。仏教を守護する菩薩としても崇められる八幡はその代表例です。寺院の境内に神社が建てられたのは、神道と仏教を一つにまとめるためでした。このことは、単一の宗教にこだわらず、複数の宗教を受け入れる日本人の信仰のあり方をよく表しています。

Connections between Shinto and Buddhism

Why do Japanese go to both shrines and temples?

Basically Japanese are not exclusive when it comes to religion. *Kami*, Buddhas and other spirits have *riyaku*—powers and benefits that can be passed on to human beings. So, most Japanese do not hesitate to pray to Shinto *kami* for health, visit Buddhist temples at New Years and be married in a Christian-style wedding ceremony. They see no conflict in this at all.

However, it is important to realize that participation in such actions is rather casual. Participating in these various "religious" events does not require a commitment to a particular belief or to a particular sect of a religion. You simply ask for help, benefit or protection or express gratitude by means of prayer, ritual, chanting or visiting a place of worship. Throughout history, Japanese have done this. They are simply maintaining that tradition.

Why are a shrine and a temple sometimes found in the same place?

When Buddhism was introduced to Japan in the 7th century, Japanese almost immediately began to try to find a way to relate buddhas and deities. The local *kami* were seen as protectors of Buddhism. By the 10th century, Shinto deities were taken to be incarnations of buddhas and bodhisattvas. By the 13th century, deities of many major shrines were identified with particular Buddhist deities.

Out of this developed the concept called *honji suijaku*, "original essence, descended manifestation." This means that Shinto deities are Japanese manifestations of buddhas. The best example is the Shinto deity Hachiman, who was taken to be a bodhisattva protecting Buddhism. Shrines were built at temples bringing the two religions together. This "cooperation" is an example of how Japanese tend to accept multiple forms of religion, rather than choosing just one.

5 禅

❓ こんな質問をされたら？

1 Is there a difference between Buddhism and Zen Buddhism?

仏教と禅宗には違いがあるのですか？

---

2 Is there a symbol of Zen Buddhism?

禅宗の特徴は何ですか？

---

3 How has Zen Buddhism influenced modern Japan?

禅宗は現代日本にどのような影響を与えていますか？

Zen

💬 **30秒で、こう答えよう！**

1 Zen is one of the branches of Buddhism.

禅宗とは仏教の一派です。

2 A stone garden in Zen temples, known as a *sekitei*, is a symbol of Zen Buddhism.

禅寺には、石庭という石造りの庭があります。

3 Habits developed in the practice of Zen Buddhism are still an important part of Japanese values. For example, Japanese people value silence, and often complain about people who talk too much.

禅によって発展した習慣は今なお日本人の重要な価値観を形成しています。たとえば、日本人は今でも沈黙に価値を置き、しゃべりすぎる人をよく批判します。

6 侍

❓ こんな質問をされたら？

1 Are there still samurai in modern Japan?

いまの日本にはまだサムライがいるのですか？

2 What were samurai?

侍とは何だったのですか？

3 What did samurai do in their daily lives?

侍は日常何をしていたのですか？

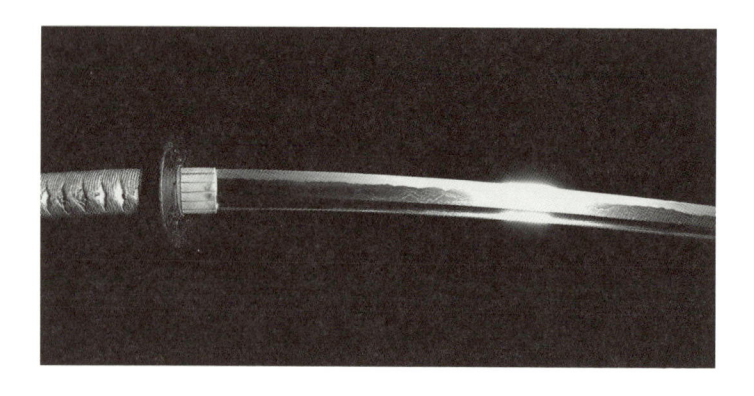

Samurai

💬 30秒で、こう答えよう！

1 No, the era of samurai ended when the government of the Tokugawa Shogunate was overthrown in 1868.

いいえ、徳川幕府が1868年に転覆されたとき、侍の時代もまた終焉を迎えました。

2 Samurai were also called bushi. Bushi means "warrior," while samurai literally means "one who serves."

侍は武士とも呼ばれました。武士は戦士を意味します。一方、侍は仕える人を意味します。

3 Samurai had to undergo rigorous training, and they also studied philosophy and ethics in order to reach a level of cultural refinement.

侍は厳格な訓練を行い、ある水準の教養を身に付けるために哲学や道徳を学ばなければなりませんでした。

7 城

❓ こんな質問をされたら？

1 Why were castles built in Japan?

なぜ日本では城が建てられたのですか？

2 Are there any differences between Japanese castles and European ones?

日本の城とヨーロッパの城には違いがあるのですか？

3 What is Japan's most famous castle?

日本でいちばん有名な城は何ですか？

Castles

💬 30秒で、こう答えよう！

1 Castles were built for military purposes from ancient times up until the medieval period. During the era of the Tokugawa Shogunate, castles served as administrative centers for local lords.

古代から中世にかけて、城は軍事目的のために築かれました。徳川幕府の時代には、城は地方の君主のための行政府になりました。

2 The main difference is that in Japan only the base ramparts of the castle were made from stone. The buildings were all wooden, and covered with thick clay and plaster to defend against fire and attack.

ヨーロッパの城との大きな違いは、城壁だけが石で築かれているということです。建物はすべて木造で、火災や攻撃から守るために粘土や漆喰を厚く塗ってあります。

3 The beautiful Himeji-jo (White Heron Castle) in Hyogo Prefecture is probably the most famous. It was originally completed in 1610, and was designated as a World Heritage Site in 1993.

兵庫県で1610年に完成した美しい姫路城（白鷺城）です。1993年に世界文化遺産に登録されています。

8 侘び・寂び・幽玄

❓ こんな質問をされたら？

1 What is "*wabi*"?

「侘び」とは何ですか？

2 What is "*sabi*"?

「寂び」とは何ですか？

3 What is "*yugen*"?

「幽玄」とは何ですか？

Wabi · Sabi · Yugen

💬 30秒で、こう答えよう！

1 *Wabi* refers to the concept of finding beauty in simplicity and frugality. For example, in the traditional tea ceremony people choose a plain setting and use plain tools to carry out the ceremony.

侘びとは、美を簡潔で質素なものとする概念です。たとえば、茶道では素朴な茶器や道具を選んで茶会を楽しみます。

---

2 *Sabi* refers to the concept of finding beauty in things that are changing or are faded. For example, old stones covered with moss are often used in Japanese gardens based on the concept of *sabi*.

寂びとは、移ろい消えてゆくものに、どのように美を見出すかということです。たとえば、苔むした古石がよく寂びの概念に従って日本庭園に使われます。

---

3 *Yugen* refers to the concept of mysterious uncertainty that's communicated from beyond death, an ultimate eternity.

幽玄とは、死を乗り越えたところにある究極の永遠から伝わる神秘的な不確実性の概念です。

第3章

日本の食

1 寿司

❓ こんな質問をされたら？

1 What is *chirashi-zushi*?

ちらし寿司とは何ですか？

2 What is *kaiten-zushi*?

回転寿司とは何ですか？

3 What is the proper way to eat sushi?

寿司の正しい食べ方とは？

Sushi

💬 30秒で、こう答えよう！

1 *Chirashi-zushi* is a style of sushi. It is prepared by covering vinegared rice with various types of raw fish, along with cooked vegetables, mushrooms and eggs.

ちらし寿司とは寿司の一形式で、酢飯の上にいろいろな種類の刺身、調理された野菜、キノコ、玉子などをのせたものです。

2 *Kaiten-zushi* refers to sushi restaurants that serve various types of sushi on conveyor belts. At the end of the meal, the waiters count the number of plates you have finished in order to calculate your bill. Different-color plates represent different prices.

回転寿司では、いろんな種類の寿司をのせた小さな皿がベルトの上を廻っています。会計のときにウエイターがテーブルの上の皿の数を数えます。皿の色によって値段が違います。

3 When eating sushi, be careful not to dip the piece too deeply into the dish of soy sauce. It is safer to flip your piece of sushi over, and dip the fish side into the soy sauce, in order to keep the rice from falling apart.

寿司を食べるときは、あまり醤油につけすぎないように注意しましょう。形を壊さないためにも、寿司をひっくり返して、魚の部分を醤油につけるのが安全です。

2 刺身

❓ こんな質問をされたら？

1 What is sashimi?

刺身とは何ですか？

2 What is the proper way to eat sashimi?

刺身の正しい食べ方とは？

3 Are there any recommendations for what to drink with sashimi?

刺身に合う飲み物を教えてください。

Sashimi

💬 30秒で、こう答えよう！

1 Sashimi is thinly sliced raw seafood, arranged attractively on a plate.

刺身は薄く切られた生魚で、皿の上にきれいに盛りつけられています。

2 Sashimi is eaten by dipping it in soy sauce that's been mixed with grated *wasabi*.

刺身はおろしたわさびと一緒に醤油につけて食べます。

3 Sashimi goes very well with Japanese sake.

刺身には日本酒がよく合います。

第3章 日本の食

3 天婦羅

❓ こんな質問をされたら？

1 What is tempura?

天婦羅とは何ですか？

2 How is tempura prepared?

天婦羅はどのように調理されますか？

3 What is the proper way to eat tempura?

天婦羅の正しい食べ方は？

Tempura

💬 30秒で、こう答えよう！

1 Tempura refers to deep-fried seafood and vegetables that have been coated with batter made from flour and eggs.

天婦羅とは、揚げた魚や野菜のことで、小麦粉と卵でできた衣でおおわれています。

2 To make good tempura, the freshest ingredients are deep-fried until they are just fully cooked, but not overcooked.

いい天婦羅を味わうためには、最も新鮮な素材をよく火が通るまで揚げなければなりませんが、揚げ過ぎてもダメです。

3 When eating tempura, you can dip each piece into a dipping sauce called *tentsuyu*, which is made from fish broth, soy sauce and *mirin* (sweet cooking sake).

天つゆというたれにつけて食べます。天つゆは、魚だし、醤油、甘口の料理酒である味醂でできています。

4 焼き鳥

❓ こんな質問をされたら？

1 What is *yakitori*?

焼き鳥とは何ですか？

2 Where can I try it?

どこで食べられますか？

3 How do I order *yakitori*?

どのように注文すればいいですか？

知っておくと便利な焼き鳥メニュー

yakitori やきとり・焼鳥 grilled chicken	shōniku 正肉 boneless meat with skin
shio 塩 (grilled with) salt	uzura うずら quail (egg)
tare タレ (grilled with) sauce	negi ねぎ・葱 leek
momo もも chicken thigh meat	shishitō ししとう small Japanese green pepper
negima ねぎま・ネギ間 chicken pieces and leek	ginnan 銀杏・ぎんなん ginkgo nut
sasami 笹身・ささみ chicken breast meat	shiitake 椎茸・しいたけ shiitake mushroom
teba 手羽 chicken wing	piiman ピーマン green pepper (often stuffed)
tebasaki 手羽先 chicken wing or wing tip	jidori 地鶏 heritage-breed chicken or hybrid
tsukune つくね minced chicken patty	torisashi 鳥刺し raw chicken
kawa かわ・皮 chicken skin	Nagoya kōchin 名古屋コーチン Cochin, an heirloom breed chicken
bonjiri ぼんじり fatty chicken tail	shamo 軍鶏 a game bird with slightly chewy meat
seseri せせり chicken neck meat	kamo 鴨 wild duck
rebā レバー liver	aigamo 合鴨 a cross between wild duck and domesticated duck
sunagimo 砂肝 gizzard	suzume すずめ sparrow (or young chicken)
sunazuri 砂ずり・砂ズリ gizzard	horohorochō ホロホロ鳥 guinea fowl
hatsu はつ・ハツ heart	

Yakitori

💬 30秒で、こう答えよう！

1 *Yakitori* is chicken grilled on skewers. It is a good example of the charms of Japan's so-called "B-class" cuisines.

焼き鳥とは、串に刺して焼いた鳥のことです。日本のB級グルメの魅力を伝える一品です。

2 You can get skewers of chicken to take home from department-store food halls, supermarkets or even convenience stores, but the best *yakitori* is served at *izakaya*-style pubs, grilled to order, preferably over good-quality charcoal.

デパートの食品売り場やスーパーマーケット、あるいはコンビニでも持ち帰ることができます。でも、最高の焼き鳥は、注文を受けてから——望むべくは高品質の炭火で——焼いてくれる居酒屋で出されるものです。

3 You can specify the cuts of the bird that you want, and whether you prefer your skewer grilled with salt (*shio*) or with sauce (*tare*).

自分の食べたい鶏の部位を注文することができます。そして、塩かタレか好みの味付けを選ぶことができます。

5 とんかつ

❓ こんな質問をされたら？

1 What is *tonkatsu*?

とんかつとは何ですか？

2 What kinds of *tonkatsu* are served in restaurants?

とんかつ屋ではどのようなとんかつが食べられますか？

3 What condiments go best with *tonkatsu*?

とんかつに合う薬味は何ですか？

Tonkatsu

💬 30秒で、こう答えよう！

1 *Tonkatsu* refers to deep-fried pork cutlets.

とんかつは豚肉を揚げたものです。

2 *Tonkatsu* restaurants offer both deep-fried fillets (called "*hire*") and pork-loin cutlets (called "*rosu*"), all at reasonable prices.

とんかつ屋でフィレとロースを揚げたものを手頃な値段で食べることができます。

3 Condiments typically include strong mustard, salt, lemon, and *tonkatsu* sauce, a thicker version of Worcestershire sauce.

薬味には、ふつう、強めの辛子、塩、レモン、濃いめのウスターソースであるとんかつソースが出されます。

6 懐石

❓ こんな質問をされたら？

1 What is *kaiseki*?

懐石とは何ですか？

2 How does one order *kaiseki*?

懐石はどのように注文すればいいですか？

3 What makes *kaiseki* special?

懐石の特徴は？

Kaiseki

30秒で、こう答えよう！

1 *Kaiseki* is a very formal style of Japanese cuisine, and it is generally served in a formal setting.

懐石は最も正式な日本料理であり、改まった席などで供されます。

2 *Kaiseki* is always served as a full-course meal, so you can't order a la carte. You can, however, choose from different price levels for full-course meals. *Kaiseki* is one of the most expensive types of Japanese cuisine.

懐石はコース料理なので、コースメニューから選びます。単品での注文はできません。懐石は最も高額な和食の一つです。

3 *Kaiseki* puts a great emphasis on seasonal ingredients and garnishes, so you can enjoy seasonal variations as well as elegant presentation.

懐石では、季節ごとの素材や付け合わせが取り入れられているので、見た目の美しさだけでなく、旬の味わいを楽しむことができます。

7 うなぎ

❓ こんな質問をされたら？

1 What is *unagi*?

うなぎとは何ですか？

2 Where can I eat *unagi*?

どこでうなぎを食べられますか？

3 Is there a best time of year to try *unagi*?

うなぎの旬はいつですか？

Unagi

💬 30秒で、こう答えよう！

1 *Unagi* is fresh-water eel, and it is prepared by grilling it in a special sauce. *Unagi* is high in protein and fats, and rich in Vitamins A and E.

うなぎは淡水魚で、特別のタレをつけて焼かれます。うなぎには豊富なタンパク質、脂肪、ビタミンA、Eが含まれています。

2 *Unagi* is served almost exclusively at *unagi* specialty restaurants.

うなぎはほとんどうなぎ専門店で供されます。

3 Japanese people eat *unagi* especially in the summertime, and it is believed that it helps the body withstand hot weather.

日本人は夏にうなぎを食べます。というのは、うなぎは暑い天候に打ち勝つ精力をつけてくれると信じられているからです。

8 そば

❓ こんな質問をされたら？

1 What is soba?

そばとは何ですか？

2 Where can I try soba?

どこでそばを食べられますか？

3 What kinds of soba are served in restaurants?

そば屋にはどんなそばがありますか？

Soba

💬 30秒で、こう答えよう！

1 Soba refers to thin buckwheat noodles.

そばは、そば粉でできた細い麺です。

2 Soba is generally served in restaurants called *soba-ya* that specialize in soba.

そば屋という専門店で食べられます。

3 Soba is served in many different styles, but the best way to appreciate the delicate flavor of the noodles is to order *mori-soba* (plain, cold noodles), or *ten-zaru* (cold noodles served with tempura).

いろいろな種類がありますが、そばの繊細さを味わうには、もりそばや天ざるがおすすめです。

9 ラーメン

❓ こんな質問をされたら？

1 What is ramen?

ラーメンとは何ですか？

2 What is it made from?

ラーメンの材料は何ですか？

3 How popular is ramen in Japan?

ラーメンは日本でどのくらい人気があるのですか？

Ramen

💬 30秒で、こう答えよう！

1 Ramen is a noodle dish that's usually served in soup. While the dish is originally from China, ramen in Japan has developed its own distinctive flavor.

汁にはいった麺料理です。中国が起源ですが、日本のラーメンは独自に味を進化させました。

2 Ramen noodles are made from wheat, and the soup can be made from various ingredients, including pork, fish, chicken, seaweed, mushrooms and vegetables.

ラーメンの麺は小麦粉で作られています。出汁は、鶏、豚、魚、昆布、キノコ、野菜などさまざまな素材からできています。

3 Ramen is extremely popular in Japan, with many famous ramen shops throughout the country. Ramen enthusiasts are known to visit ramen shops quite often.

ラーメンは日本で大人気で、全国に有名店があります。有名店を定期的に訪問するような熱狂的なファンが大勢います。

10 カレーライス

❓ こんな質問をされたら？

1 What is Japanese curry?

日本のカレーって何ですか？

2 Where can I try it?

どこで食べられますか？

3 Is there any particular type of curry that you would recommend?

どんなカレーがおすすめですか？

Curries

💬 30秒で、こう答えよう！

1 Curries are a part of Indian cuisine, but Japanese people have developed their own distinctive version of this dish. Japanese curry is served as "curry rice," which is curry sauce on top of steamed rice.

> カレーはインド料理ですが、日本人は独自のものを作りました。日本のカレーは蒸した米の上にカレーソースをかけた「カレーライス」として出されます。

2 Curry specialty restaurants can be found in cities throughout Japan.

> 日本には多くのカレーライス専門店があります。

3 The most popular type is beef curry, while *katsu* curry (deep-fried pork cutlets with curry sauce) is also very popular among Japanese people.

> ビーフカレーが一番人気ですが、カツカレーも日本人に人気があります。

11 お好み焼き

❓ こんな質問をされたら？

1 What is *okonomiyaki*?

お好み焼きとは何ですか？

2 What is it made from?

材料は何ですか？

3 Are there different styles of *okonomiyaki*?

どんな種類がありますか？

Okonomiyaki

💬 30秒で、こう答えよう！

1 *Okonomiyaki* is a savory pancake made with various ingredients added to a pancake batter.

お好み焼きはパンケーキの生地にさまざまな素材を入れた香ばしいパンケーキのことです。

2 *Okonomiyaki* is made with a wide range of ingredients, starting with diced seafood and meat, various chopped vegetables and a variety of toppings.

お好み焼きには、さいの目に刻まれた魚介や肉から、みじん切りにされた野菜など、実に幅広いトッピングがあります。

3 In the Hiroshima area a layer of wheat noodles is usually added to *okonomiyaki* in addition to the many other ingredients.

広島では、多くの素材に加えて、焼きそばがお好み焼きにミックスされます。

12 どんぶりもの

❓ こんな質問をされたら？

1 What is *donburi*?

丼とは何ですか？

2 What types of *donburi* dishes are there?

どんな種類がありますか？

3 What is *oyako-don*?

親子丼とは何ですか？

Donburi

💬 30秒で、こう答えよう！

1 *Donburi*, or rice-bowl dishes, are a popular style of fast food in Japan.

丼は日本で人気のファーストフードです。

2 The most popular types of rice-bowl dishes are *oyako-don*, *katsu-don*, *ten-don* and *gyu-don*.

人気の丼料理は、親子丼、カツ丼、天丼、牛丼です。

3 *Oyako-don* is a rice-bowl dish topped with chicken and covered with onions and egg.

親子丼は鶏肉をのせ、玉ねぎと卵でおおった丼です。

13 弁当

❓ こんな質問をされたら？

1 What is a bento?

弁当とは何ですか？

2 Where can I try a bento?

どこで食べられますか？

3 What is an *ekiben*?

駅弁とは何ですか？

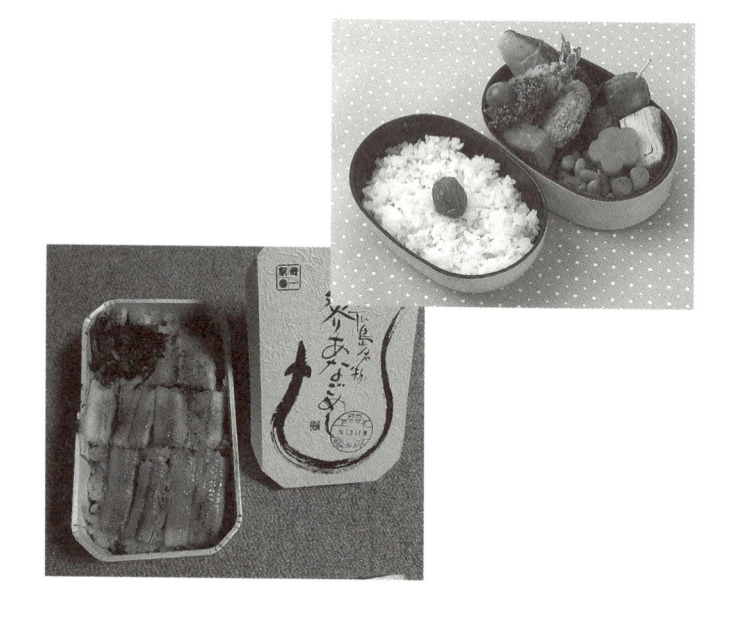

Bento

💬 **30秒で、こう答えよう！**

1 A bento is a boxed lunch.

弁当とは箱に入れたランチのことです。

---

2 At lunchtime, many upscale Japanese restaurants offer beautifully arranged mini-*kaiseki* dishes in a lacquer box.

高級和食店のなかには、昼食時に美しく仕上げたミニ懐石料理を漆塗りの箱に入れて出すところもあります。

---

3 *Ekiben* refers to bento boxes that are sold at train stations, and they usually include local specialty dishes.

駅弁とは列車の駅で売られている弁当のことで、地元の特産物が入っています。

14 梅干し・わさび・鰹節

❓ こんな質問をされたら？

1 What is an *umeboshi*?

梅干しとは何ですか？

---

2 What is *wasabi*?

わさびとは何ですか？

---

3 What is *katsuobushi*?

鰹節とは何ですか？

Umeboshi · Wasabi · Katsuobushi

💬 30秒で、こう答えよう！

1 An *umeboshi* is a pickled plum. It's very sour, and it is said to be good for one's health.

梅干しは、梅の実を漬けたもので、とても酸っぱく健康にいいものです。

---

2 *Wasabi* is Japanese horseradish. It is usually served with raw fish because it has sterilizing properties.

わさびとは日本のホースラディッシュのことで、殺菌作用があるのでふつうは刺身についてきます。

---

3 *Katsuobushi* is dried, smoked bonito. People shave or slice it to use it in soup stock and to flavor many Japanese dishes.

鰹節は干して燻したカツオのことで、削ったり細切りにして、汁物の出汁や多くの料理の味付けに使います。

第3章 日本の食

15 お茶

❓ こんな質問をされたら？

1 Is it true that green tea is free at restaurants in Japan?

日本のレストランではお茶が無料で振る舞われるって本当ですか？

2 Do Japanese people perform a tea ceremony whenever they drink tea?

日本人はお茶を飲むときには必ず茶道をおこなうのですか？

3 Where can I find green tea?

緑茶はどこで手に入りますか？

Ocha

💬 **30秒で、こう答えよう！**

1 Japanese people call green tea *ocha,* and it is usually free in restaurants, just as water is.

日本人はグリーンティーのことをお茶といい、レストランではふつう水のように無料です。

2 The tea used in the tea ceremony is called *matcha.* It's a powdered tea that's different from the type of tea served on ordinary occasions.

茶会で点てられるお茶は抹茶という粉末状のもので、日常出されるお茶とは違います。

3 These days Japanese people enjoy bottled cold tea, which is sold in vending machines.

昨今、日本人はペットボトルに入った冷たいお茶を飲みますが、これは自動販売機で買えます。

16 和菓子

❓ こんな質問をされたら？

1 What is *wagashi*?

和菓子とは何ですか？

2 What is *anko*?

あんことは何ですか？

3 What is the most popular type of *wagashi* in Japan?

日本でいちばん人気のある和菓子は何ですか？

Wagashi

💬 30秒で、こう答えよう！

1 *Wagashi* is a traditional type of Japanese confectionery. Sophisticated, beautifully decorated *wagashi* are a common element of the tea ceremony.

和菓子とは伝統的な日本のお菓子のことです。洗練され、きれいに仕上げられた和菓子は、茶会の儀式には欠かせないものです。

2 *Anko* is Japanese red-bean paste.

あんことは日本の伝統的な小豆のあんのことです。

3 *Sembei* rice crackers are the most popular type of *wagashi*. They are made from rice flour, with seasonings and other ingredients added for flavor.

煎餅が最も人気のある和菓子です。煎餅は米粉と味付けのための材料で作られています。

17 酒

❓ こんな質問をされたら？

1 What is sake?

酒とは何ですか？

2 Is it common in Japan to pour sake into someone else's glass?

日本ではお酒を注いであげるのが普通なのですか？

3 What does "*kanpai*" mean?

「乾杯」とは何ですか？

Sake

💬 30秒で、こう答えよう！

1 Sake is a traditional alcoholic beverage made from rice. It is often called "rice wine" in English.

酒は米からできた日本の伝統的なアルコールです。酒のことを英語ではよく「ライスワイン」といいます。

2 If you are drinking with Japanese friends, it is common practice for people to pour sake or beer into each other's glasses.

日本人の友人と一緒であれば、酒やビールを相手のコップに注いであげるのはふつうのことです。

3 *"Kanpai"* simply means "Cheers!". People say it to make a toast.

乾杯とは英語でいう「Cheers」のことです。祝杯をあげるときにいいます。

18 焼酎

❓ こんな質問をされたら？

1 What is *shochu*?

焼酎とは何ですか？

2 Do you have any advice on how to drink *shochu*?

焼酎はどのように飲めばいいのですか？

3 What is *awamori*?

泡盛とは何ですか？

Shochu

💬 30秒で、こう答えよう！

1 *Shochu* is a distilled alcoholic beverage made using rice, wheat, potatoes or sugar.

焼酎は日本の蒸留酒で、米、麦、芋、黒糖などから造られています。

2 You can drink *shochu* on the rocks, and many *shochu* cocktails have recently become popular. You can enjoy it mixed with fresh fruit juices such as lemon and grapefruit, or even mixed with green tea.

オンザロックで飲めますが、最近では焼酎カクテルがたくさん生み出されています。レモンやグレープフルーツといった新鮮な果実やお茶で割ってもいけますよ。

3 *Awamori* is a type of *shochu* produced in the Okinawa area. It is mainly made from Indica rice, which is mostly imported from Thailand.

泡盛は沖縄で造られる有名な焼酎で、ほとんどがタイから輸入されたインディカ米で造られます。

第4章

日本の風物

1 花見

❓ こんな質問をされたら？

1 Why do Japanese people love cherry blossoms so much?

なぜ日本人は花見がこれほど好きなのですか？

2 What is "*sakura zensen*"?

「桜前線」とは何ですか？

3 Is there a name for the custom of gathering under the cherry blossoms to have a picnic?

桜の下で宴会する習慣を何ていうのですか？

Hanami

💬 30秒で、こう答えよう！

1 Because cherry blossoms are regarded as a symbol of the transient nature of the world, blooming briefly and then quickly falling.

なぜかというと、咲いたと思えばすぐに散る、そんな桜は浮世の儚さを象徴するものとみなされているからです。

2 *Sakura zensen* is the front line showing where cherry blossoms have just started to open. It represents the arrival of spring, traveling from south to north.

桜前線とは、桜が開花する前線のことです。それは南から北上してくる春の到来を告げてくれます。

3 This custom is called "*hanami*" in Japanese. It dates back about four hundred years, to the time when ordinary citizens began to enjoy cherry-blossom parties as entertainment.

この習慣は日本語で花見といわれ、約400年前に一般庶民の娯楽として広まりました。

第4章　日本の風物

2 満員電車

❓ こんな質問をされたら？

1 When is Tokyo's notorious morning rush hour?

東京の悪名高い朝のラッシュアワーはいつですか？

2 How crowded are the trains and subways?

電車や地下鉄はどのくらい混雑するのですか？

3 Why are trains and subways still so crowded even late at night?

なぜ電車や地下鉄は夜遅くまで混むのですか？

Rush Hour

💬 30秒で、こう答えよう！

1 Tokyo's public transportation hits the peak of morning rush hour between eight and nine a.m., and it is terribly crowded during that period.

たいてい午前8時から9時の間に、公共交通はたいへん混み合います。

2 Tokyo residents are used to being pushed into subway cars, standing so close to other commuters that they are touching.

東京の人は、ラッシュ時に地下鉄などに押し込まれ、体と体をくっつけながら通勤することに慣れています。

3 Many people work overtime or socialize with friends or colleagues after work, so they don't head home until late.

というのも、多くの人が、残業したり、仕事終わりに人付き合いをしているから、遅くまで帰宅しないのです。

3 新幹線

❓ こんな質問をされたら？

1 What is the Shinkansen?
新幹線とは何ですか？

2 How fast is it?
どのくらいの速さですか？

3 When would you use it?
どんなときに使うのですか？

Shinkansen

💬 30秒で、こう答えよう！

1 Shinkansen is the name of the Japanese high-speed train network and the trains that run on it. They are often called bullet trains because of their shape.

新幹線とは日本の高速列車網とそこを走る列車の名称です。新幹線はその姿形からよく弾丸列車と呼ばれます。

2 Shinkansen trains can reach speeds of 300 kilometers per hour, and can travel between Tokyo and Fukuoka in around five hours.

新幹線は時速 300 キロで走ります。たとえば、東京と福岡を約 5 時間で結びます。

3 Shinkansen trains are especially convenient for travel between the cities of Tokyo, Nagoya, Kyoto and Osaka. Trains between these cities run every fifteen minutes or so.

特に便利なのが、東京、名古屋、京都、大阪を移動するときに新幹線を利用することです。というのも、これらの都市間へは 15 分間隔で便があるからです。

4 電子マネー

❓ こんな質問をされたら？

1 Are there any special passes that can be used on public transportation?

公共交通を使うときに定期券のようなものはありますか？

2 How do I buy one of these?

どうやって買うことができますか？

3 Can I use these passes anywhere in Japan?

日本中どこでも使うことができますか？

Prepaid Cards

💬 30秒で、こう答えよう！

1 If you use public transportation regularly, it is convenient to use a prepaid card. Two different prepaid cards, called Suica and PASMO, are used in Tokyo.

公共交通機関を定期的に利用する場合、プリペイドカードを利用するのが便利です。東京では、SuicaとPASMOの2種類のカードが使われています。

2 Visitors from abroad can buy Suica or PASMO cards at station kiosks or at "Green Window" ticket reservation windows at most subway and train stations. A 500-yen deposit is required.

外国から来た人も、駅のキオスクや切符を予約する「みどりの窓口」で500円の供託金を支払い、PASMOやSuicaを購入できます。

3 Similar prepaid cards are used in major cities such as Osaka. You can use your Suica or PASMO card in these major cities as well; they're not limited to the Tokyo area.

大阪など大都市には、PASMOとSuicaと同じようなカードがあります。PASMOとSuicaは東京地区限定ではなく、これら東京以外の大都市でも使用できます。

5 デパ地下

❓ こんな質問をされたら？

1 What is a "*depa-chika*"?

「デパ地下」とは何ですか？

2 What do they sell?

何が売られていますか？

3 Why are they so popular?

なぜそんなに人気があるのですか？

Depa-chika

💬 30秒で、こう答えよう！

1 *Depa-chika* is an abbreviation of the Japanese term for "department-store basement."

デパートの地下のフロアを「デパ地下」といいます（文字どおり、デパートの地下の略称です！）。

2 *Depa-chika* sell a wide variety of food and drinks from all over Japan and around the world, including traditional Japanese sweets and Western-style desserts.

そこでは、日本をはじめ世界中から取り寄せたさまざまな食料品やアルコールを購入することができます。そのうえ、和洋の伝統的なお菓子も揃っています。

3 Because many foods are ready to eat and prepared to high standards, busy people can purchase food for the dinner table directly from a *depa-chika*.

多くの食品はすぐに食べることができ、高品質なので、忙しい人たちはよくデパ地下で夕食の惣菜を求めます。

6 コンビニ

❓ こんな質問をされたら？

1 How many convenience stores are there in Tokyo?

東京にはどれくらいコンビニがあるのですか？

2 What can I buy at a Japanese convenience store?

コンビニでは何が買えますか？

3 Is it open round the clock?

24時間営業ですか？

Convenience Stores

30秒で、こう答えよう！

1 There are thousands of convenience stores in Tokyo. You are usually never more than five minutes away from a convenience store.

東京には数千のコンビニがあります。東京では普通、コンビニまで5分もかかりません。

2 In addition to food, such as sandwiches, rice balls and boxed meals called bento, convenience stores also sell useful everyday items such as pens, toothbrushes and batteries.

コンビニでは、サンドイッチ、おにぎり、弁当という箱詰めされた食事などの食料が売られているだけでなく、ボールペン、歯ブラシ、電池といった日常品も売られています。

3 Most convenience stores are open 24 hours a day, seven days a week.

ほとんどのコンビニが年中無休24時間営業です。

7 温泉

❓ こんな質問をされたら？

1 What is an *onsen*?

温泉とは何ですか？

2 Are *onsens* good for your health?

温泉は健康にいいのですか？

3 Where can I experience an *onsen*?

どこで温泉を体験できますか？

Onsen

💬 30秒で、こう答えよう！

1. *"Onsen"* is the word for hot springs in Japanese. Since Japan is made up of volcanic islands, hot springs can be found throughout the country.

   ホットスプリングのことを日本では温泉といいます。日本は火山列島なので、温泉は全国にあります。

2. Yes, the waters in an onsen contain various minerals, depending on the region.

   そうです。温泉には地域によって、さまざまな種類のミネラルが含まれているのです。

3. In many cases, people stay at a *ryokan*, or a Japanese inn, to enjoy an *onsen* experience.

   多くの場合、旅館に泊まって温泉を楽しみます。

8 旅館

❓ こんな質問をされたら？

1 What is a *ryokan*?

旅館とは何ですか？

2 Do *ryokans* serve food?

旅館では食べ物が出されますか？

3 How are they different from regular hotels?

通常のホテルとどこが違うのですか？

Ryokan

💬 30秒で、こう答えよう！

1 A *ryokan* is a traditional Japanese inn. When you stay at a *ryokan* you can enjoy Japanese-style entertainment and stay in a traditional room.

旅館とは伝統的な日本の宿泊所のことです。旅館では和室で日本式の娯楽を楽しむことができます。

2 At many *ryokans*, the price of your stay includes dinner and breakfast. *Ryokans* generally offer traditional Japanese meals.

多くの旅館では、夕食と朝食は（宿泊代に）含まれています。一般的に、伝統的な和食が振る舞われます。

3 Most of the time people staying at a *ryokan* sleep on futons, which are traditional Japanese sleeping mats. The futon will be laid out in your room by an employee of the *ryokan*.

ほとんどの場合、旅館では伝統的な日本の寝具である布団で寝ることになります。布団は旅館の従業員によって部屋に敷かれます。

第4章 日本の風物

9 居酒屋

❓ こんな質問をされたら？

1 What is an *izakaya*?

居酒屋とは何ですか？

2 What is the atmosphere like in an *izakaya*?

居酒屋の中はどんな感じですか？

3 What can I drink there?

どういったものが飲めますか？

Izakaya

💬 30秒で、こう答えよう！

1 An *izakaya* is the equivalent of a pub in a Western country; it's a place where hard-working office workers can stop in on their way home after work to share a drink and light snacks with colleagues.

居酒屋とは、西洋でいうところの「バー」や「パブ」に当たります。仕事帰りに勤労者たちが立ち寄り、同僚とお酒や軽食を楽しむのです。

---

2 *Izakayas* often have traditional decor, with a counter where customers who come alone or in pairs can sit, plus tables and chairs for groups of customers, or tatami mats.

居酒屋には伝統的な室内装飾が施され、ふつうは、一人客や二人客が酒を飲むために木製のカウンターがあり、グループ客にはテーブル席が用意されます。座敷のある店もあります。

---

3 The selection of beverage is often quite broad, and normally includes draft beer. Some *izakaya* specialize in Japanese sake or *shochu*.

飲み物はかなり広く揃えられています。通常、樽から注がれる生ビールはもちろんのこと、なかには日本酒や焼酎に特化した居酒屋もあります。

10 だるま

❓ こんな質問をされたら？

1 What is a *daruma*?

だるまとは何ですか？

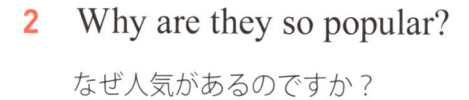

2 Why are they so popular?

なぜ人気があるのですか？

3 Where does the name "*daruma*" come from?

「だるま」という名前の由来は？

Daruma

💬 30秒で、こう答えよう！

1 *Daruma* dolls are legless, armless and neckless dolls made from wood, plastic, stone or paper mache over a bamboo frame, and they can be seen all over Japan.

手足や首のないだるまは、木やプラスティックや石、または竹棒を用いた張り子でつくる人形で、日本各地で目にすることができます。

2 Because, for Japanese people, they symbolize the spirit of never giving up. They often have a rounded, weighted base so that they will always roll back upright when they get tipped over.

なぜなら、日本人はだるまを不屈の精神を表すものと見なしているからです。だるまの多くは、底が重くて丸い形をしているので、倒しても必ず起き上がるのです。

3 The name comes from the Indian Buddhist priest Boddhidharma, the founder of Zen Buddhism.

名前の由来は、インドの禅僧で禅宗の開祖、菩提達磨です。

11 招き猫

❓ こんな質問をされたら？

1 What is that ornamental cat with a raised paw?

あの手を挙げている猫の飾りは何ですか？

2 Why are they displayed?

なぜ飾られているのですか？

3 Is there a difference between a raised right paw and a raised left paw?

右手をあげているのと左手をあげているのと違いがあるのですか？

Maneki-neko

💬 30秒で、こう答えよう！

1 It's called a *maneki-neko*, a beckoning cat, and it can be made of clay, porcelain, paper mache, wood or plastic.

招き猫です。粘土、磁器、張り子、木、プラスティックなどからできています。

2 Because they are good-luck talismans, traditionally believed to bring success to shops and restaurants. They are also often displayed as a sign of welcome in the *genkan* entrance of houses.

なぜなら、開運のお守りとして、商店やレストランに商売繁盛を招くと信じられているからです。訪問客を歓迎する印として、一般家庭の玄関にもよく置かれています。

3 Those with a raised right paw are believed to bring good luck in business, while those with a raised left paw are for welcoming customers or guests.

右の前脚をあげている招き猫は金運を、左の前脚をあげている招き猫は客を招くとされています。

12 タクシー

❓ こんな質問をされたら？

1 Are taxis in Japan safe?

日本のタクシーは安全ですか？

2 Where can I hail a taxi?

どこでタクシーを拾えますか？

3 How can I tell if a taxi is vacant?

どうしたらタクシーが空車かどうかわかりますか？

Taxis

💬 30秒で、こう答えよう！

1 Taxi fares are based on a metered system, so you don't have to worry about being overcharged.

タクシーはメーター制なので、過剰請求される心配はありません。

2 Except in a few special areas, you can hail a taxi anywhere just by waving your hand. In areas like Ginza, taxis line up at taxi stands.

タクシーは、一部の地区を除いて、どこでも手をあげれば乗ることができます。銀座などでは、タクシーはタクシー乗り場に並んでいます。

3 An illuminated sign in the corner of the front window tells you if the taxi is vacant or not. If the sign is red, the taxi is vacant.

フロントウインドウの角にある空車表示灯でそのタクシーが空車か否かがわかります。表示が赤のときは空車です。

13 オタク文化

❓ こんな質問をされたら？

1 What is *otaku* culture?

オタク文化とは何ですか？

2 How widespread is *otaku* culture?

オタク文化はどれくらい広まっているのですか？

3 What is the original meaning of "*otaku*" in Japanese?

「オタク」の本来の意味は何ですか？

Otaku Culture

💬 30秒で、こう答えよう！

1 *Otaku* culture represents Japanese pop culture in the form of animation, manga, and the lifestyles of young people.

オタク文化は、アニメ、マンガといった日本のポップカルチャーや若者のライフスタイルの象徴です。

2 *Otaku* culture is the culture of the Japanese computer age, and it spread throughout the world as manga became popular.

オタク文化は日本のコンピュータ世代が生み出した文化で、マンガが知られるようになると、世界にも広がっていきました。

3 The original meaning of the word "*otaku*" is "your house." In the past, it was considered rude to call other people by their personal names, so instead people referred to one another by the place or direction they came from.

オタクのもともとの意味は、"あなたの家"です。昔は、相手のことを名前で呼ぶのは失礼だとされていました。その代わりに場所ややってきた方向で、互いを呼びました。

14 コスプレ

❓ こんな質問をされたら？

1 What is cosplay?

コスプレとは何ですか？

2 How did cosplay become famous around the world?

どうやってコスプレは世界中で人気になったのですか？

3 Where is the mecca of cosplay?

コスプレの聖地はどこですか？

Cosplay

💬 30秒で、こう答えよう！

1 Cosplay is an activity in which people wear costumes and put on makeup to imitate characters from animation, games and manga.

コスプレとは、アニメ、ゲーム、マンガなどのキャラクターを真似て、コスチュームを着て、化粧をしたりすることです。

2 Since Japanese animation, manga and computer games are very popular with young people around the world, cosplay from Japan also spread to many countries.

日本のアニメ、マンガ、コンピュータゲームが世界中の若者に人気があるため、メイドインジャパンのコスプレも多くの国に広まっています。

3 Akihabara is the hub of *otaku* and cosplay culture in Tokyo.

東京の秋葉原が、オタク、コスプレ文化の中心です。

15 歌謡曲

❓ こんな質問をされたら？

1 What is J-pop?

Jポップとは何ですか？

2 How has it evolved in Japan?

日本でどのように進化したのですか？

3 What is *enka*?

演歌とは何ですか？

Popular Music

💬 30秒で、こう答えよう！

1 J-pop is an abbreviation for Japanese popular music, and it is popular not only in Japan but in many Asian countries as well.

> Jポップは、ジャパニーズ・ポップ・ミュージックの略で、日本だけでなく、多くのアジアの国々でも人気があります。

2 After the Second World War, many types of popular music were introduced to Japan, and were combined with Japanese traditional popular music.

> 第二次世界大戦後、多くのポップミュージックが日本に紹介され、日本にある昔からの音楽と結びつきました。

3 *Enka* is a genre of Japanese popular music with a traditional folk flavor. *Enka* songs are often about love, passion, and the spirit of life in Japan.

> 演歌は、大衆音楽のジャンルのひとつで、日本古来の民謡の影響があります。演歌で歌われるのは、愛、情念、日本の心などです。

第5章

日本の伝統文化

1 歌舞伎

❓ こんな質問をされたら？

1　What is kabuki?

歌舞伎とは何ですか？

2　Why do male performers play both men's and women's roles?

なぜ男性の役者が男も女も演じるのですか？

3　Where can I see a kabuki performance?

どこで歌舞伎を鑑賞できますか？

Kabuki

💬 30秒で、こう答えよう！

1 Kabuki is a Japanese performing art developed during the Edo period.

歌舞伎は江戸時代に発展した日本の舞台芸術です。

2 Originally, women performed in kabuki plays, but the shogun banned them from performing because kabuki was considered to be sexually provocative.

本来、歌舞伎は女性が演じるものでしたが、幕府が、性的な挑発になるということで、女性が演じることを禁止したのです。

3 In Tokyo, kabuki performances can be seen at the Kokuritsu Gekijo, or National Theater, and at the Kabuki-za. You can enjoy kabuki performances with English translations at both those venues.

東京で歌舞伎が行われるのは国立劇場か歌舞伎座ですが、英語の翻訳付きで楽しむことができます。

2 能

❓ こんな質問をされたら？

1 What is *noh*?

能とは何ですか？

2 What are some features of *noh*?

能の特徴は？

3 What is the mask that performers wear?

能楽師がつけている面は何ですか？

Noh

💬 30秒で、こう答えよう！

1 *Noh* is a classical type of performing art in Japan. *Noh* developed from *sarugaku*, a combination of traditional folk dance, comedy and stage drama from medieval times.

能は日本の古典的な舞台演劇です。能は猿楽から発展した、中世の踊り、コメディ、舞台劇などが混ざったものです。

---

2 *Noh* is a performing art known for its minimal, slow movement. Many people consider *noh* to be quite sophisticated in its minimalism.

能は、最小限のゆっくりとした動きで行われる舞台芸術です。多くの人は能はそのミニマリズムゆえに、洗練されていると言います。

---

3 It is a called a *noh-men*. *Noh* actors wear masks, and they can create many facial expressions with the masks by changing angles, light and shadow.

能面といいます。能の役者は面をつけ、面の角度による光や影を利用して、様々な顔の表情を作り出します。

3 狂言

❓ こんな質問をされたら？

1　What is *kyogen*?

狂言とは何ですか？

2　How is *kyogen* different from noh?

狂言は能とどのように違うのですか？

3　What are some important features of *kyogen*?

狂言の特徴とは？

Kyogen

💬 30秒で、こう答えよう！

1 *Kyogen* refers to the comedy performances between noh plays.

狂言は能の演目の間に演じられる滑稽劇です。

2 Unlike noh, *kyogen* is usually performed without masks.

能と違って、ほとんどの狂言は面を着けることはありません。

3 *Kyogen* is based on ordinary stories from everyday life, and actors use colloquial language.

狂言は日常生活のよくある話がベースで、役者も口語で話します。

4 いけばな

❓ こんな質問をされたら？

1 What is *ikebana*?

いけばなとは何ですか？

2 What are some important features of *ikebana*?

いけばなの特徴は？

3 Which school of *ikebana* is the biggest in Japan?

日本最大のいけばなの流派は？

Ikebana

💬 30秒で、こう答えよう！

1 *Ikebana* is the traditional Japanese art of flower arrangement. *Ikebana* is also known as *kado*.

いけばなは日本の伝統的なフラワーアレンジメントのことです。いけばなのことを華道ともいいます。

2 *Ikebana* can be considered to be a spatial art, because flower arrangements are created based on the relationship between the lines of the flowers and the spaces between them.

いけばなが空間の芸術と言われるのは、空間と花のラインを組み合わせるものだからです。

3 *Ikenobo* is the biggest school of flower arranging in Japan.

池坊が、日本最大の華道の流派です。

5 茶道

❓ こんな質問をされたら？

1 What is *sado*?

茶道とは何ですか？

2 What is the purpose of *sado*?

茶道の目的は？

3 Are there special rules of etiquette for *sado*?

茶道の礼儀には特別な決まりがあるのですか？

Sado

💬 30秒で、こう答えよう！

1 *Sado* refers to the tea ceremony, a traditional ritual in which tea is prepared and served.

茶道は伝統的な儀式で、そこでは茶を点てて楽しみます。

---

2 The tea ceremony is an artistic practice meant to create a refined environment in which to serve tea to important visitors.

茶道は大切な客をもてなすために、洗練された雰囲気をつくり出すための芸術です。

---

3 Formal tea-ceremony etiquette is very complicated. There are rules that cover how to walk, how to move your hands, how to sit and so on.

礼儀に適った茶道の所作は複雑です。歩き方、手の動かし方、座り方などに及びます。

Column 茶の湯

Tea Utensils 茶道具

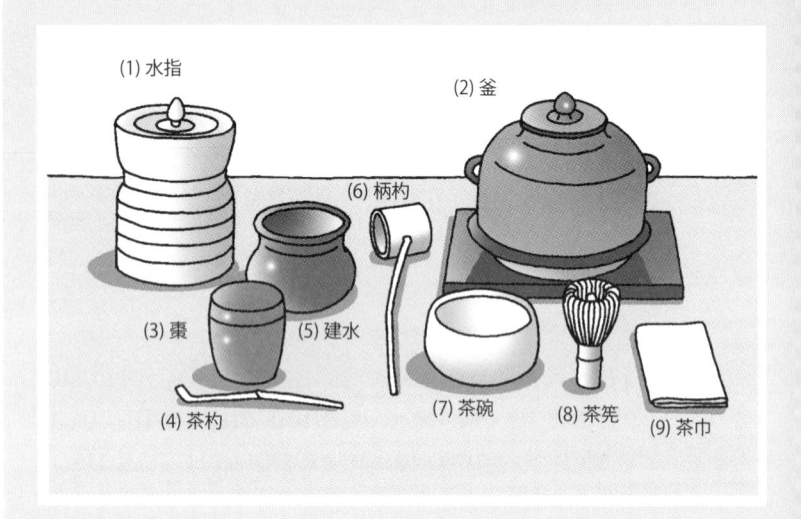

(1) 水指
(2) 釜
(3) 棗
(4) 茶杓
(5) 建水
(6) 柄杓
(7) 茶碗
(8) 茶筅
(9) 茶巾

(1) *mizusashi,* Jug of water

(2) *kama,* Kettle and brazier

(3) *natsume,* Lacquerware container for powdered green tea

(4) *chashaku,* Tea scoop, used to transfer powdered tea from the natsume to the teabowl

(5) *kensui,* Basin for used water

(6) *hishaku,* Water ladle

(7) *chawan,* Teabowl

(8) *chasen,* Split bamboo tea whisk, used to whip the powdered tea with water

(9) *chakin,* Tea cloth

Tea Ceremony

Tearoom 茶室

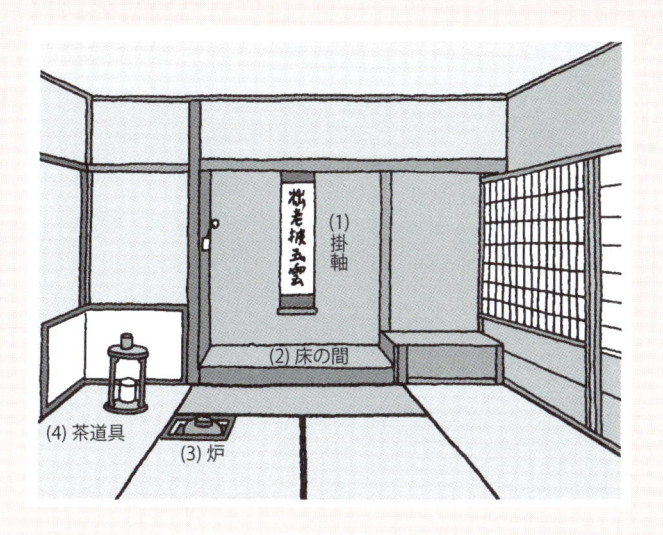

(1) 掛軸
(2) 床の間
(3) 炉
(4) 茶道具

(5) 床の間
(7) 水屋
(6) 炉
(8) 次の間
(9) 入口
(10) 上座 ↑
(11) 下座 ↓

(1) *kakejiku*, Scroll
(2) (5) *tokonoma*, Alcove
(3) (6) *ro*, Hearth
(4) *chadogu*, Tea utensils
(7) *mizuya*, Room for tea and food preparation
(8) *tsuginoma*, Afterroom
(9) *iriguchi*, Main entrance, used by the guests
(10) *kamiza*, Top seat
(11) *shimoza*, Lower seat

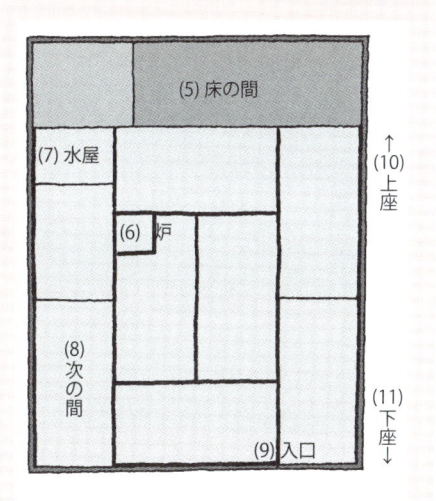

第5章 日本の伝統文化

Taking Your Seat 席入りの手順

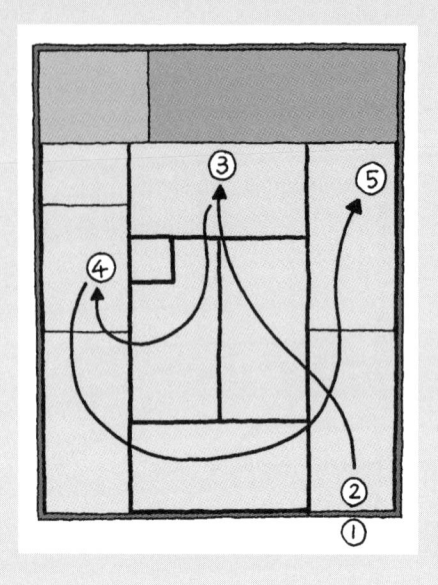

① 入り口の襖を開け、扇子を前に置いて、かるく会釈

Open the *fusuma* at the entrance, place your fan (*sensu*) in front, and bow slightly.

② にじって敷居を越す

Edge forward over the threshold.

③ 床正面に座り、かるく手をついて掛物を拝見

Sitting in front of the alcove, place your hands lightly on the *tatami*, and admire the hanging scroll.

④ 道具畳に座り、釜、炉縁を拝見

Sitting in the afterroom, admire the kettle and brazier.

⑤ 正客の座に進み、足を揃えて座る

Proceed to the position for the first guest and sit with legs arranged properly.

⑥ 亭主を迎え、挨拶をする

Greet the host with a bow.

Making the Tea お茶を点てる

① 入り口に座り、一礼

Sitting in the entrance, bow as a sign of respect.

② 炉の前に座り、茶道具を揃える

Sit in front of the hearth and arrange the utensils.

③ 茶碗、茶筅を前に置く

Place the teabowl and whisk in front of you.

④ いちど茶碗にお湯を入れ、建水に捨ててから、茶碗を拭く

Pour hot water into the teabowl, empty the water into the basin for that purpose, and wipe the teabowl.

⑤ お茶を2杓すくい、茶碗に入れる

Scoop two spoonfuls of powered tea into the teabowl.

⑥ 柄杓でお湯を茶碗に入れる

Ladle hot water into the teabowl (3.5 ladlefuls).

⑦ お茶を点てる

Whisk the teabowl into a fine froth.

⑧ 茶碗の正面を客に向けて出す

Facing forward, offer the teabowl to the guest.

第5章 日本の伝統文化

Drinking the Tea お茶の飲み方

① お茶が出されると、茶碗をとって、膝前に仮置きする

Pick up the teabowl and place it in front of your knees.

② 正客の座に戻り、茶碗を次客との間において。「お先に」と次礼する

Return to your position and place the bowl between yourself and the second guest, saying, "Pardon me [for drinking before you]."

③ 茶碗をとり、感謝の気持ちを込めておしいだく

Taking up the bowl, drink for the first time with a feeling of gratitude.

④ 茶碗を手前に2度回して、正面を左横に向けて、3口半ほどで飲みきりする

Rotate the bowl once, and with the front of the bowl facing to the left, first take a sip and then finish the rest.

⑤ 飲み口を親指と人差し指で左から右へ拭く

With your thumb and index finger, wipe from left to right the place where your lips touched the bowl.

⑥ 茶碗を拝見する

Admire the bowl.

⑦ 茶碗の正面を向こうに回してから返す

Rotate the teabowl so that the front is facing away from you and return it to the host.

6 相撲

❓ こんな質問をされたら？

1 What is *sumo*?

相撲とは何ですか？

2 Why do *sumo* wrestlers throw salt?

なぜ関取は塩をまくのですか？

3 Why do *sumo* wrestlers stamp their feet?

なぜ関取は四股を踏むのですか？

Sumo

💬 30秒で、こう答えよう！

1 *Sumo* is the sport of traditional Japanese wrestling. It originally developed as a special style of wrestling that was performed to worship gods and goddesses.

相撲とは、日本の伝統的なレスリングのことです。相撲はいろいろな神を崇拝するための特別な取組として発展しました。

2 In the wrestling ring (which is called the "*dohyo*"), *sumo* wrestlers throw salt to ward off evil spirits.

土俵の上で、力士は塩を投げ、邪悪なものを取り払います。

3 In the *dohyo*, *sumo* wrestlers stamp their feet in order to drive into the ground the bad air that causes diseases and disaster.

土俵上で、力士は四股を踏みますが、これは病気や不幸などの悪い気を地下に押し込めるためです。

7 盆栽

❓ こんな質問をされたら？

1 What is *bonsai*?

盆栽とは何ですか？

2 What are some important features of *bonsai*?

盆栽の特徴とは？

3 Why is *bonsai* so popular among older people?

なぜ盆栽は高齢者の間で人気があるのですか？

Bonsai

💬 30秒で、こう答えよう！

1 *Bonsai* refers to the cultivation of miniature potted trees. It involves an interesting combination of manipulation of nature while encouraging an appreciation of nature.

盆栽とは、ミニチュア鉢植え栽培のことです。自然そのものへの敬意を促す一方で自然を操る、興味深い融合の世界です。

2 The idea behind *bonsai* is to create dwarf versions of trees with a totally natural look.

木々の小型版をつくりあげるという発想のもと、完全に自然な趣をかもし出します。

3 Because *bonsai* can live for hundreds of years, their image of immortality makes them popular with the elderly.

なぜなら、盆栽は何百年も生き続けるので、この不朽のイメージが年配者層を魅了するのです。

8 浮世絵

❓ こんな質問をされたら？

1 Why were ukiyo-e produced?

なぜ浮世絵がつくられたのですか？

2 What is *shunga*?

春画とは何ですか？

3 What were the most famous ukiyo-e works?

最も有名な浮世絵作品は何ですか？

Ukiyo-e

💬 30秒で、こう答えよう！

1 Ukiyo-e prints were the equivalent of modern-day picture postcards, posters and pin-ups, as well as book illustrations.

浮世絵版画は、今日の絵葉書、ポスター、ブロマイドや本の挿絵に相当するものだったのです。

2 *Shunga* were erotic prints, meant for both entertainment and instruction.

春画とは、エロティックな版画のことで、娯楽と教育を兼ねたものでした。

3 Among the most famous works are Hiroshige's "53 Stages of Tokaido," Hokusai's "36 Views of Mt. Fuji," Sharaku's "Kabuki Actors," and Utamaro's "Beauties."

広重の「東海道五十三次」や北斎の「富嶽三十六景」、写楽の役者絵、歌麿の美人画などが有名です。

第5章 日本の伝統文化

第6章

日本の都市

1 東京

❓ こんな質問をされたら？

1 What is the capital of Japan?
日本の首都はどこですか？

2 How many people live in Tokyo?
東京の人口は？

3 How large is Tokyo's economy?
東京の経済規模は？

Tokyo

💬 30秒で、こう答えよう！

1 It's Tokyo, which is also the center of government, including the legislature and the judiciary.

東京です。東京はまた、日本の行政、立法、そして司法の中心地でもあります。

2 The population of Tokyo is 13 million. More than 30 million people live in the greater Tokyo area.

東京には、1300万人の人が住んでいます。東京とその周辺を合わせると、3000万人の人が住んでいます。

3 Tokyo's GDP (Gross Domestic Product) is around 92.9 (ninety-two point nine) trillion yen. Tokyo's economy is around half the size of California's economy.

東京都の都内総生産は約92兆9000億円です。その経済規模は、カリフォルニア州の半分です。

2 京都

❓ こんな質問をされたら？

1 Where is Kyoto located?

京都はどこにありますか？

2 What are some noteworthy features of Kyoto?

京都の知っておくべき特徴は？

3 Where would you recommend walking in Kyoto?

京都を散策するのにおすすめの場所は？

Kyoto

💬 30秒で、こう答えよう！

1 Kyoto is located around 460 kilometers west of Tokyo. It takes two hours and fifteen minutes to travel from Tokyo to Kyoto on the Shinkansen.

京都は東京の西、460キロのところに位置してます。東京から京都までは、新幹線で2時間15分かかります。

2 Kyoto is not only a former capital, but it is also the country's cultural heart. In Kyoto you can enjoy countless historical sites such as old temples with beautiful gardens, shrines, villas and traditional houses.

京都は古都ということだけでなく、日本の文化の中心です。美しい庭のある古い寺、神社、別荘、伝統的な家など、数えきれない名所旧跡が京都にはあります。

3 Gion is a national historical preservation district where you can see many old houses, tea houses (called *ochaya*) and restaurants.

祇園は国の歴史保存地区で、古くからの民家、お茶屋、料理屋などがあります。

第6章 日本の都市

3 大阪

❓ こんな質問をされたら？

1 Where is Osaka located?

大阪はどこにありますか？

2 What are some noteworthy features of Osaka?

大阪の特徴は？

3 Where is the commercial center of Osaka?

大阪の繁華街は？

Osaka

💬 30秒で、こう答えよう！

1 Osaka is a city located about 550 kilometers west of Tokyo. It takes around two hours and thirty minutes to travel from Tokyo to Osaka by Shinkansen.

大阪は東京から550キロ西のところに位置しています。東京と大阪の間は、新幹線で2時間半かかります。

2 Osaka people are proud of their sense of humor, and they have developed their own style of comedy.

大阪では、自分たちのユーモアのセンスに誇りを持っていて、独特のお笑いエンターテインメントがあります。

3 Nanba is Osaka's biggest commercial center, and it is located south of Osaka Station.

難波が大阪最大の繁華街で、大阪駅の南側に位置してます。

4 奈良

❓ こんな質問をされたら？

1 Where is Nara located?

奈良はどこにありますか？

2 What are some noteworthy features of Nara?

奈良の特徴は？

3 What would you recommend seeing in Nara?

奈良のおすすめのスポットは？

Nara

💬 30秒で、こう答えよう！

1 Nara Prefecture is located at the center of the Kii Peninsula, and Nara City is the capital. Nara is easy to visit from Kyoto; it takes only thirty minutes by train from Kyoto Station.

奈良県は紀伊半島の真ん中あたりに位置し、奈良市が県庁所在地です。奈良は京都から簡単に行けます。電車で京都駅から30分ほどです。

2 Nara is one of the most famous ancient cities in Japan, and it was the capital of Japan from 710 to 792. Compared with Kyoto, the atmosphere of Nara is very relaxed.

奈良は日本でも指折りの歴史の町で、710年から792年の間、都が置かれていたところです。京都と比べると、奈良はかなりリラックスした雰囲気です。

3 In Nara, you should visit Todai-ji Temple, which was built in the eighth century. Todai-ji Temple is famous for housing the world's largest bronze Buddha statue, which was completed in 752.

奈良では8世紀に建立された東大寺に行くのがよいでしょう。東大寺は、752年に完成した世界最大の銅製の大仏で有名です。

5 広島

❓ こんな質問をされたら？

1 Where is Hiroshima located?

広島はどこにありますか？

2 What are some noteworthy features of Hiroshima?

広島の特徴は？

3 What would you recommend seeing in Hiroshima?

広島で見るべきものは？

Hiroshima

💬 30秒で、こう答えよう！

1 Hiroshima Prefecture is located in the Chugoku Region of western Honshu island. It takes around four hours and thirty minutes to reach Hiroshima from Tokyo by Shinkansen.

広島県は、本州の西に位置する中国地方にあります。東京から広島までは、新幹線で4時間半です。

2 Hiroshima is known around the world as the site of an atomic bombing in 1945. The atom bomb destroyed the city and killed more than 200,000 people.

広島は、1945年に原爆で破壊されたことから、世界中で知られています。20万人以上の人が広島の原爆で亡くなりました。

3 There are two UNESCO World Heritage Sites in Hiroshima Prefecture. One is the Hiroshima Peace Memorial Park, and the other is Itsukushima Shrine.

広島県には、世界遺産が2つあります。ひとつは広島平和記念公園で、もうひとつが厳島神社です。

6 福岡

❓ こんな質問をされたら？

1 Where is Fukuoka located?

福岡はどこにありますか？

2 What are some noteworthy features of Fukuoka?

福岡の特徴は？

3 What would you recommend seeing in Fukuoka?

福岡で見るべきものは？

Fukuoka

💬 30秒で、こう答えよう！

1 Fukuoka Prefecture is located in the northern part of Kyushu, which is the southernmost of Japan's four major islands. You can travel to Fukuoka directly from Tokyo on the Shinkansen. It takes around five hours.

福岡は、日本列島の主要4島のなかで最南端に位置する九州の北部にあります。福岡まで東京から新幹線で行けます。約5時間です。

2 From Fukuoka Airport, you can fly to many Asian countries. There is also hovercraft service between Fukuoka and the city of Busan in South Korea.

福岡空港からは、アジア各地へ飛行機で行くことができます。福岡と韓国の釜山の間には、ホバークラフトが運行しています。

3 The downtown area of Fukuoka is called Hakata, and you can experience local traditions there. Hakata is the merchant area of Fukuoka, and every summer a festival called Yamagasa takes place there.

福岡の下町、博多には地元気質や伝統が残っています。博多は福岡の商業地域で、山笠という夏祭りもここで行われます。

7 沖縄

❓ こんな質問をされたら？

1　Where is Okinawa located?

沖縄はどこにありますか？

2　What is the history of Okinawa?

沖縄の歴史とは？

3　What is the biggest current issue in Okinawa?

沖縄で今いちばんの問題は何ですか？

Okinawa

💬 30秒で、こう答えよう！

1 Okinawa is located midway between Kyushu and Taiwan. It is spread out over 160 islands in the southern portion of the Ryukyu Islands. The capital city is Naha.

沖縄は九州と台湾の間に位置しています。沖縄は、160の島が連なる琉球諸島の南にあり、その県庁所在地は那覇です。

2 Okinawa was once an independent country called the Ryukyu Kingdom. In 1945, Okinawa was attacked by the United States and became a brutal battlefield.

沖縄はかつては琉球王国という独立国でした。1945年、沖縄はアメリカ軍に攻撃され、激しい戦場となりました。

3 Based on the Japan-US Security Treaty, many US military bases are located on the main island of Okinawa. For Japanese people, the issue of US bases in Okinawa, which occupy 18 percent of the main island, is a controversial political matter.

日米安全保障条約により、沖縄本島にはたくさんの米軍基地があります。日本人にとって、沖縄本島の18％を占める米軍基地の問題は、賛否両論ある政治的関心事です。

8 北海道

❓ こんな質問をされたら？

1 Where is Hokkaido located?

北海道はどこにありますか？

2 What are some noteworthy features of Hokkaido?

北海道の特徴は？

3 What would you recommend seeing in Hokkaido?

北海道で見るべきものは？

Hokkaido

💬 30秒で、こう答えよう！

1 Hokkaido is one of the four major islands of Japan, and it is located just north of Honshu.

北海道は日本の4つの主な島のうちのひとつで、本州のすぐ北に位置しています。

2 Winters are very cold in Hokkaido, and there are many ski resorts there. On the eastern shore of Hokkaido you can enjoy the beautiful site of gigantic ice floes washing ashore.

北海道の冬はとても寒く、スキーリゾートもたくさんあります。北海道の東側の沿岸には大量の流氷が流れ着き、見事です。

3 Sapporo is the capital and commercial center of Hokkaido. There is a snow festival held in Sapporo every year in early February, where you can enjoy the sight of snow sculptures on display outdoors.

札幌は北海道の道庁所在地であり、商業の中心です。札幌では2月初旬に雪祭りが行われ、野外にディスプレイされた雪の像などを楽しめます。

第6章 日本の都市

9 銀座

❓ こんな質問をされたら？

1 Where is Ginza located?

銀座はどこですか？

2 What are some noteworthy features of Ginza?

銀座の特徴は？

3 What would you recommend seeing in Ginza?

銀座の見所は？

Ginza

30秒で、こう答えよう！

1 Ginza is a neighborhood in Tokyo's Chuo Ward. Ginza is also the name of a stop on the Ginza, Hibiya and Marunouchi subway lines.

銀座は東京都の中央区にあります。銀座には銀座線、日比谷線、丸ノ内線などの地下鉄が停車します。

2 Ginza is a shopping and entertainment district. It has some of the most expensive real estates in Tokyo. Ginza also has some of the most expensive restaurants and bars in the city.

銀座はショッピングや娯楽の街です。銀座は東京でも最も地価の高いところです。銀座は東京でも最も高価なレストランやバーのある街です。

3 Ginza has department stores such as Mitsukoshi, and designer boutiques for brands like Chanel. Chuo Street is closed to traffic on weekend afternoons, turning it into a so-called "pedestrian heaven."

銀座には三越などいくつかの百貨店があり、シャネルのようなブランドショップもあります。週末、中央通りは歩行者天国になり、車をしめだします。

10 浅草

❓ こんな質問をされたら？

1 Where is Asakusa located?

浅草はどこですか？

2 What are some noteworthy features of Asakusa?

浅草の特徴は？

3 What would you recommend seeing in Asakusa?

浅草の見所は？

Asakusa

💬 30秒で、こう答えよう！

1 Asakusa is a neighborhood in the northeast side of central Tokyo. Asakusa Station is the terminal station of the Ginza subway line.

浅草は、東京の北東の地域にある街です。浅草は地下鉄銀座線の終点に位置しています。

---

2 Asakusa is one of several Tokyo neighborhoods that have kept a nostalgic atmosphere.

浅草は、東京の中でも昔の情緒の残る地域の一つとして知られています。

---

3 Asakusa is the home of Senso-ji, Tokyo's most famous temple. Near Asakusa there is an area called Kappabashi where shops sell restaurant supplies, including plastic food models.

浅草には、浅草寺という有名な寺があります。浅草の近くに合羽橋という通りがあって、プラスチック製の料理のサンプルなど、レストランの道具を扱う店が並んでいます。

第6章 日本の都市

Column 合羽橋道具街・浅草寺

合羽橋道具街

Very close to Asakusa is a shopping area called Kappabashi, which is famous for its many shops selling cooking utensils and supplies for the restaurant business. Japanese cuisine is enjoying a global boom, and it has been recognized as part of Japan's cultural heritage. These days not only Japanese shoppers but also many shoppers from abroad visit the Kappabashi area, where they shop for distinctive Japanese kitchen knives and other unique utensils for preparing Japanese food. Plastic food models, which are often displayed in the windows of restaurants to give patrons an idea of the food served inside, are another item popular with Kappabashi shoppers.

　浅草のそばにある合羽橋道具街は、調理道具やレストラン用品を扱う店がずらりとならぶ場所として知られています。最近の和食ブームで、海外の人も多くこの場所を訪れ、和包丁や和食用の調理道具などを買い求めます。日本のレストランなどで展示されるプラスチックで作った食品サンプルなども人気の商品です。

Kappabashi Kitchen Town & Senso-ji

浅草寺

Senso-ji which is the oldest Buddhist temple in Tokyo, is considered to be a symbol of the Asakusa area. The temple houses a statue of the Bodhisattva Kannon, a treasured Buddhist relic, which is not open to public view.

Senso-ji is located in the center of Asakusa, and reportedly the entire compound of temple buildings, including a monastery, was already in place by the tenth century. Between the main Kaminari-mon entrance of the compound and the temple, with its stunning five-story pagoda, visitors walk down a very crowded street that's lined with "*naka-mise*" shops selling souvenirs and food. This whole area is known as the "*Monzen-machi*" – a small town in itself that lies within the area of the temple compound. The temple, the pagoda and this entire bustling neighborhood were destroyed during bombings in World War II, but they were rebuilt shortly after the war.

浅草の象徴ともいわれる浅草寺は、東京最古の寺で、観音菩薩を祀っています。ただし、本尊は秘仏とされ、一般には公開されていません。

浅草寺は浅草の中心に位置し、10世紀には寺院としての伽藍が整えられたといわれています。表参道の入り口にある雷門から、お寺の境内に至る参道にある門前町は、仲見世と呼ばれ、お土産物屋がずらりと並んでいます。本堂や五重の塔は第二次世界大戦で焼失したため、戦後に再建されたものです。

第7章

東京サバイバル

1 地下鉄を乗りこなす

1

Q Where does the Ginza Line run?

銀座線はどこを走っていますか？

A The Ginza Line runs from Asakusa to Shibuya by way of Ginza, and it is Japan's oldest subway line.

銀座線は、浅草から銀座を経て渋谷を結ぶ、日本で最も古い地下鉄です。

2

Q Where does the Fukutoshin Line run?

副都心線はどこを走っていますか？

A The Fukutoshin Line is connected to the Toyoko Line, so you can ride all the way to Yokohoma without changing trains.

地下鉄副都心線に乗れば、そのまま東横線に直通し乗り換えなしに横浜まで行くことができます。

3

Q Where does the Tozai Line run?

東西線はどこを走っていますか？

A The Tozai Line connects Chiba Prefecture with central Tokyo, and then continues on to the Chuo and Sobu train lines.

東西線は、千葉県と都心を結び、さらに中央・総武線へと乗り入れています。

4

Q Where does the Marunouchi Line run?

丸ノ内線はどこを走っていますか？

A The Marunouchi Line is a useful subway line that runs more or less in a loop from Ikebukuro to Shinjuku by way of Otemachi, Tokyo Station and Ginza. From Shinjuku it continues west to Ogikubo or Honancho.

丸の内線は、池袋から大手町、東京駅、銀座を経由して新宿までぐるりとまわってゆく便利な地下鉄です。丸ノ内線は、新宿から西に向かって荻窪、または方南町へとつづきます。

5

Q Where does the Chiyoda Line run?

千代田線はどこを走っていますか？

A The Chiyoda Line is a subway line that runs as a continuation of the JR Joban train line. It runs past the front of the Imperial Palace and then to Yoyogi Uehara, where it continues as the Odakyu train line.

千代田線は JR 常磐線からの直通運転で運行されている地下鉄です。皇居の前を通り、代々木上原という駅で、小田急線に乗り入れています。

6

Q Where does the Hibiya Line run?

日比谷線はどこを走っていますか？

A The Hibiya Line is a subway line that continues on from the Tobu Isesaki Line in the north and the Tokyu Toyoko Line in the south.

日比谷線は、北は東武伊勢崎線、南は東急東横線と直通運転している地下鉄です。

7

Q Where does the Yurakucho Line run?

有楽町線はどこを走っていますか？

A The Yurakucho Line is a subway line that continues on from the Seibu Ikebukuro Line and the Tobu Tojo Line in the north. It runs from Ikebukuro to Shin-Kiba, next to Tokyo Bay, by way of Nagatacho and Ginza.

有楽町線は、北部で西武池袋線や東武東上線と直通運転している地下鉄です。池袋から永田町や銀座を経て東京湾に近い新木場まで運行しています。

8

Q Where does the Hanzomon Line run?

半蔵門線はどこを走っていますか？

A The Hanzomon Line is a subway line that continues on from the Tobu Isesaki Line in the east. It runs through central Tokyo and continues as the Tokyu Denentoshi Line in the west of Shibuya.

半蔵門線は、東は東武伊勢崎線と直通運転している地下鉄です。都心を経由したあと、西は渋谷から東急田園都市線に乗り入れています。

9

Q Where does the Nanboku Line run?

南北線はどこを走っていますか？

A The Namboku Line is a subway line that continues on from the Tokyu Meguro Line in the west. It runs from south to north through central Tokyo and continues north to Saitama Prefecture.

南北線は、西は東急目黒線に乗り入れている地下鉄です。都心を南北に横断したあと、埼玉県へとのびています。

10

Q Where does the Toei Mita Line run?

都営三田線はどこを走っていますか？

A The Toei Mita Line is a subway line that runs north from Mita to the residential area of Takashimadaira by way of Yurakucho and Otemachi.

都営三田線は、三田駅から北へ向かって有楽町や大手町を経て、高島平という住宅街へのびる地下鉄です。

11

Q Where does the Toei Shinjuku Line run?

都営新宿線はどこを走っていますか？

A The Toei Shinjuku Line is a subway line that connects with the Sobu Line in the east. It runs from Chiba through central Tokyo and joins the Keio Line at Shinjuku, running to the residential area of Tama in the west.

都営新宿線は、東は総武線と直通する地下鉄です。千葉から都心を経て、新宿から京王線に乗り入れて、西は多摩地区という住宅地へとのびています。

12

Q Where does the Toei Oedo Line run?

都営大江戸線はどこを走っていますか？

A The Toei Oedo Line is a loop subway line that runs around central Tokyo, with one spur running northwest to an area called Hikarigaoka.

都営大江戸線は、都心部を周回する地下鉄の環状線で、支線は北西に向かい、光が丘という地区につながります。

2 JRを乗りこなす

1

Q Where does the Yamanote Line run?

山手線はどこを走っていますか？

A The Yamanote Line is a loop line that connects major train stations in central Tokyo. Major stops on the Yamanote Line are Tokyo, Ueno, Ikebukuro, Shinjuku, Shibuya and Shinagawa.

山手線は、都心部の主要駅を繋ぐ環状線です。山手線の沿線の主要駅には、東京、上野、池袋、新宿、渋谷、品川などがあります。

2

Q Where does the Chuo Line run?

中央線はどこを走っていますか？

A The Chuo Line runs west from Shinjuku Station through Kofu and Matsumoto to Nagoya. Rapid trains on the Chuo Line run from Tokyo Station by way of Shinjuku Station to Hachioji and Takao.

中央線は、新宿駅から西に伸び、甲府や松本を経て、名古屋へつながっています。中央線には、東京駅から新宿を経て八王子や高尾を結ぶ快速が運行されています。

3

Q Where does the Keihin Tohoku Line run?

京浜東北線はどこを走っていますか？

A During the daytime, rapid trains on the JR Keihin Tohoku Line connect Omiya, Tokyo, Yokohama and Ofuna.

京浜東北線は、大宮と東京、横浜、さらに大船を結ぶJR路線で、昼間は一部快速運転をしています。

4

Q Where does the Chuo-Sobu Line run?

中央・総武線はどこを走っていますか？

A The Chuo-Sobu Line is a JR train line that runs from Mitaka in the west to Chiba, by way of Shinjuku and Akihabara.

中央・総武線は、西の三鷹を起点に新宿、秋葉原を経て千葉を結ぶJRの路線です。

3 成田空港 vs 羽田空港

1

Q How many international airports are there in the Tokyo area?

東京には国際空港がいくつありますか？

A The Tokyo area has two international airports, Haneda and Narita.

東京には羽田と成田の二つの国際空港があります。

2

Q How are Narita and Haneda airports different?

成田と羽田空港の違いは？

A Tokyo's main international gateway is Narita Airport. Domestic flights and some international flights arrive at and depart from Haneda Airport.

東京の国際線の玄関口は主に成田空港です。羽田空港では、国内便や一部の国際線が発着します。

3

Q How do I get to Narita Airport?

成田空港へはどうやっていけますか？

A There are two main ways to get to and from Narita Airport by train.

First, the Keisei Skyliner train departs from Keisei Ueno and Nippori stations, and takes around 40 minutes to get to Narita Airport.

Second, a limited express train called the Narita Express goes to Narita Airport from Tokyo Station and takes about one hour. In addition to Tokyo Station, the Narita Express stops at several other major stations around the city.

成田空港へは 2 路線でアクセスできます。

アクセス 1；成田空港へは京成上野駅と日暮里駅から、京成スカイライナーという電車が便利です。東京都内から成田空港まで、京成スカイライナーで約 40 分かかります。

アクセス 2；東京駅からは成田エクスプレスという特急列車が成田空港に向かっています。東京駅から成田空港まで、成田エクスプレスで約 1 時間かかります。成田エクスプレスは、東京とその周辺の主な駅からも利用できます。

4

Q Are there limousine buses to Narita Airport?

成田空港へはリムジンバスが走っていますか？

A Limousine buses run to Narita Airport from the Hakozaki Bus Terminal (Tokyo City Air Terminal) in Tokyo. Limousine buses also run from major hotels in Tokyo. Without traffic, it takes around 80 minutes to get to Narita Airport by limousine bus.

東京には箱崎というバスターミナルがあり、成田空港までのリムジンバスが発着しています。東京の主要なホテルからも成田空港へはリムジンバスが運行しています。成田空港へのバスでの所要時間は、渋滞がなければ 80 分前後です。

成田空港

5

Q Can you tell me how to get to Haneda Airport?

羽田空港への行き方を教えてくれませんか？

A A monorail line runs from Hamamatsucho Station to Haneda Airport. It takes thirty minutes to get to Haneda from Hamamatsucho. You can also reach Haneda Airport from central Tokyo by taking the Keikyu Railway. The Keikyu Railway connects directly with the Toei Asakusa subway line. If you take an express train on the Keikyu Railway you can get to Haneda Airport from central Tokyo in around thirty minutes.

羽田空港へは浜松町駅からモノレールがでています。浜松町から羽田空港までの所要時間は約30分です。都心から羽田空港には京急電鉄でも行くことができます。京急電鉄は都営浅草線と直通しています。京急電鉄の急行にのれば、都心から約30分で羽田空港に着きます。

羽田空港

4 東京の歩き方

1

Q Why does the Tokyo address system sound very confusing!

なぜ東京の住所表示はとても複雑なのですか？

A Because most streets in Tokyo don't have names. Instead of by street names, Tokyo addresses are determined by block numbers. That's why many hotels, restaurants and shops have maps on their websites.

なぜならば、東京の通りにはほとんど名前がついていないからです。名前ではなく、住居番号で住所が決められているのです。それで、多くのホテルやレストラン、そしてショップはウエブサイトに地図を載せています。

2

Q What are the raised yellow strips on the ground?

地面で見かける黄色の突起物は何ですか？

A You can see raised yellow strips on sidewalks and on the floors of train stations; they are there to help blind people get around.

歩道や駅には、地面に黄色い盛り上がったストライプの表示がありますが、これは、目の不自由な人が利用するためのものです。

3

Q Why is music played at some intersections?

交差点で音楽が流れているのはなぜですか？

A At some intersections, music is played when the light changes in order to help blind people know when to cross the street.

交差点のなかには、信号が変わるときに音楽が流れるところがあります。これは目の不自由な人に渡るタイミングを教えているのです。

5 治安

1

Q What is the crime rate in Japan?

日本の犯罪率は？

A Compared to other countries, Japan has a low crime rate and is fairly safe.

Police boxes, called "*koban*" in Japanese, can be found throughout Japan, and they can help you in case of emergency.

日本は他の国々に比べると犯罪率が低く、安全です。日本中に、交番という警察官が待機している詰所があり、緊急のときに援助をしてもらうことができます。

2

Q What should I do if I lose something?

失くしものをしたらどうすればいいですか？

A You should go to a police box.

交番に行きましょう。

3

Q How do you call the police?

警察の連絡先は？

A If you need to call the police, dial 110.

警察に連絡をしなければならないときは、110番に電話しましょう。

4

Q How do you call an ambulance?

救急車を呼ぶには？

A If you need to call an ambulance or the fire department, dial 119.

救急車や消防車を呼ばなければならないときは、119番に電話しましょう。

6 郵便、キャッシング、クレジットカード

1

Q Do the ATMs at Japanese banks accept foreign cards?

日本の銀行の ATM では外国のカードは使えますか？

A No, they don't. But the ATMs in post offices and in some convenience stores do accept foreign ATM cards.

日本の銀行の ATM は外国のカードを受け付けません。しかし、郵便局やコンビニのなかには外国のカードを受け付ける ATM があります。

2

Q Are credit cards accepted in Japan?

日本ではクレジットカードは使えますか？

A These days more and more places in Japan accept credit cards.

近頃の日本では、クレジットカードを使える場所がどんどん増えてきました。

7 外国人からよく聞かれる質問

1

Q What is the best way to get around central Tokyo?

東京の中心部を移動するには何がベストですか？

A Public transportation is by far the best way to get around central Tokyo during the day. It's inexpensive, fast and very safe.

都心の昼間の移動は公共交通を利用することを強くおすすめします。公共交通は安く、迅速で、極めて安全な乗り物です。

2

Q Is sushi expensive even in Japan?

日本でも寿司は高いのですか？

A Sushi is generally thought of as an expensive food, but at "conveyor-belt sushi" restaurants, called *kaiten-zushi* in Japanese, you can enjoy sushi at a very affordable price.

寿司は一般的に高価な食べ物と思われていますが、回転寿司屋では極めて経済的に寿司を楽しめます。

3

Q Can I drink the tap water in Japan?

日本では水道水は飲めますか？

A Yes, it's fine to drink tap water in Japan.

日本の水道の水は飲んでも問題はありません。

4

Q Do I have to tip in Japan?

日本ではチップが必要ですか？

A There is no custom of tipping in Japan. If you leave a tip for someone, they might try to return your money.

日本ではチップの習慣はありません。チップを渡そうとすれば、渡された相手はそれを返そうとするでしょう。

5

Q Can I get WiFi anywhere?

WiFi はどこにでもありますか？

A Major cities like Tokyo are well covered, but you still can't get WiFi everywhere.

東京のような大都市では環境は充実していますが、どこでも WiFi を利用できるわけではありません。

6

Q I'm very tired. Can I get a massage?

疲れたのでマッサージを受けたいのですが？

A You can experience traditional Oriental Medicine in Japan. Acupuncture, moxibustion and *shiatsu* work well to relieve fatigue and muscle pain.

日本では、東洋医学を簡単に体験することができます。針やお灸、そして指圧は疲労や筋肉痛によく効きます。

7

Q Can I watch TV in English?

TV 番組に英語放送はありますか？

A Some TV programs in Japan are broadcast in multiple languages. For example it is often possible to switch Japanese news programs to English.

日本では、音声多重放送があります。日本語のニュースなどの多くも英語に切り替えて視聴できます。

8

Q Do Japanese people speak English?

日本人は英語を話しますか？

A People in Japan may be able to read and write English, but not many can actually speak English. When you speak English, it is best to speak as slowly as possible and it can also be useful to write down what you want to say.

日本では、英語の読み書きはできても、会話のできる人はそう多くはありません。英語で話をするときは、できるだけゆっくり話し、時には筆談などを交えると効果的です。

9

Q Do taxi drivers speak English?

タクシーの運転手は英語を話しますか？

A Unfortunately most taxi drivers don't speak English. You should carry a business card from your hotel to show to your taxi driver.

残念ながら、ほとんどのタクシー運転手は英語ができません。タクシー運転手に見せるために、宿泊するホテルの名刺を持っておくことをおすすめします。

10

Q How big are the capsules in capsule hotels?

カプセルホテルの部屋はどのくらいの広さですか？

A You get a space as large as a bed, with just enough overhead room to sit up.

ベッドひとつ分程度の広さと、背を伸ばして座れるくらいの高さです。

11

Q What is curry-pan?

カレーパンとは何ですか？

A Curry-pan is a deep-fried doughnut filled with curry sauce.

カレーパンとは、生地の中にカレーを詰めてよく揚げたものです。

E-CAT

English Conversational Ability Test
国際英語会話能力検定

● E-CATとは…
英語が話せるようになるためのテストです。インターネットベースで、30秒であなたの発話力をチェックします。

www.ecatexam.com

iTEP

● iTEP®とは…
世界各国の企業、政府機関、アメリカの大学300校以上が、英語能力判定テストとして採用。オンラインによる90分のテストで文法、リーディング、リスニング、ライティング、スピーキングの5技能をスコア化。iTEP®は、留学、就職、海外赴任などに必要な、世界に通用する英語力を総合的に評価する画期的なテストです。

www.itepexamjapan.com

30秒でできる！
ニッポン紹介
おもてなしの英会話

2016年8月2日　第1刷発行
2017年12月7日　第3刷発行

監修　安河内　哲也

発行者　浦　晋亮

発行所　IBCパブリッシング株式会社
〒162-0804 東京都新宿区中里町29番3号 菱秀神楽坂ビル9F
Tel. 03-3513-4511　Fax. 03-3513-4512
www.ibcpub.co.jp

印刷所　株式会社シナノパブリッシングプレス

© 2016 IBC Publishing
Printed in Japan

落丁本・乱丁本は、小社宛にお送りください。送料小社負担にてお取り替えいたします。
本書の無断複写(コピー)は著作権法上での例外を除き禁じられています。

ISBN978-4-7946-0421-7